CHARLES F. STANLEY BIBLE STUDY SERIES

DEVELOPING A SERVANT'S HEART

BECOME FULLY LIKE CHRIST
BY SERVING OTHERS

CHARLES F. STANLEY

THOMAS NELSO.
Since 1798

T0053509

DEVELOPING A SERVANT'S HEART
CHARLES F. STANLEY BIBLE STUDY SERIES

Copyright © 1996, 2008, 2020 by Charles F. Stanley.

Published in Nashville, Tennessee, by Thomas Nelson. Thomas Nelson is a registered trademark of HarperCollins Christian Publishing, Inc.

Thomas Nelson titles may be purchased in bulk for educational, business, fundraising, or sales promotional use. For information, e-mail SpecialMarkets@ThomasNelson.com.

ISBN 978-0-310-10562-6 (softcover)
ISBN 978-0-310-10563-3 (ebook)

First Printing February 2020 / Printed in the United States of America

CONTENTS

A Fresh Perspective on Serving

The Bible is more than a great piece of literature or a book of inspirational and spiritual truths. It is a practical manual for daily living. In many ways, it is God's "service manual" for life. It tells us how to live a godly life, how to maintain loving relationships, and how to fulfill our reason for being on this earth. It clearly tells us how to use our gifts, time, talents, money, and more for God's glory and His purposes.

From cover to cover, the Bible is filled with examples of men and women who had a servant's heart and who demonstrated loving service to others. Virtually all of the great stories in the Bible fall into one of three categories: (1) God's service to humankind, (2) humankind's service to God, and (3) the service of men and women to each other.

Service is giving, and giving is the essence of the gospel. God gave His only begotten Son. Jesus gave His life on the cross. We give our hearts to God. We are called to give of ourselves to others. The Bible tells us how to serve others and what to expect when we do so. It challenges us to serve with generosity and unconditional love.

This book can be used by you alone or by several people in a small-group study. At various times, you will be asked to relate to the material in one of the following four ways.

First, what new insights have you gained? Make notes about the insights you have. You may want to record them in your Bible or in a separate journal. As you reflect on your new understanding, you are likely to see how God has moved in your life.

Second, have you ever had a similar experience? You approach the Bible from your own unique background . . . your own particular set of understandings about the world that you bring with you when you open God's Word. For this reason, it is important to consider how your experiences are shaping your understanding and allow yourself to be open to the truth that God reveals.

Third, how do you feel about the material? While you should not depend solely on your emotions as a gauge for your faith, it is important for you to be aware of them as you study a passage of Scripture and can freely express them to God. Sometimes, the Holy Spirit will use your emotions to compel you to look at your life in a different or challenging way.

Fourth, in what way do you feel challenged to respond or to act? God's Word may inspire you or challenge you to take a particular action. Take this challenge seriously and find ways to move into it. If God reveals a particular need that He wants you to address, take that as His "marching orders." God will empower you to do something with the challenge that He has just given you.

Start your Bible study sessions in prayer. Ask God to give you spiritual eyes to see and spiritual ears to hear. As you conclude your study, ask the Lord to seal what you have learned so you will not forget it. Ask Him to help you grow into the fullness of the nature and character of Christ Jesus.

I encourage you to keep the Bible at the center of your study. A genuine Bible study stays focused on God's Word and promotes a growing faith and a closer walk with the Holy Spirit in each person who participates.

SAVED TO SERVE

IN THIS LESSON

Learning: What is God's purpose for our lives?
Why did He save us?

Growing: How can I become more like Christ?

Complete these three statements: (1) *God saved me because* _____, (2) *God's purpose for saving me was* _____, and (3) *I am most like Jesus when I* _____. The purpose for my opening this Bible study with a little quiz is to set the proper framework for our discussion of servanthood. The answers that I am seeking are these: (1) God saved me because *He loves me,* (2) God's purpose for saving me was *to bring Him glory,* and (3) I am most like Jesus *when I serve others.* Let's begin by looking at these three statements.

GOD SAVED ME
BECAUSE HE LOVES ME

In the opening chapter of the Gospel of John, we read, "The Word became flesh and dwelt among us, and we beheld His glory, the glory as of the only begotten of the Father, full of grace and truth" (1:14). God sent His Son, Jesus, into the world to dwell among us and live as one of us. He did this for one single reason: because He loved us and wanted to reconcile us to Himself. God forgives us, grants us eternal life, and gives us the gift of His Holy Spirit out of His immeasurable love and grace. There is no other reason.

Many people seem to believe that God saves them because of their good works or service. But nothing could be further from the truth. In fact, there isn't any type of service that can earn salvation. The apostle Paul made this clear when he chided the believers in Galatia for believing that following the Old Testament law would bring them salvation. As he wrote, "O foolish Galatians! . . . Did you receive the Spirit by the works of the law, or by the hearing of faith? Are you so foolish? Having begun in the Spirit, are you now being made perfect by the flesh? Have you suffered so many things in vain—if indeed it was in vain?" (Galatians 3:1–4).

If God saved a person on the basis of works, we would have to ask ourselves, "How much good service is enough?" Such a question cannot be answered. There is no amount of good service that can equal the shed blood of Jesus Christ. The gospel is that Jesus Christ shed His blood on the cross to purchase salvation for you and for me. He did so voluntarily and willingly in obedience to His heavenly Father. As John writes in his Gospel, "For God so *loved* the world that He gave His only begotten Son, that whoever believes in Him should not perish but have everlasting life" (3:16).

Just as people are not saved because of their past good works, neither is a person saved because they have the potential for future good works. God does not look at one person and say, "You have the potential to be a preacher, so I am going to save you," and then look at another and say, "You aren't worth much, so I won't save you." God's gift of salvation is offered freely to all who will receive it. "But as many as received Him, to them He gave the right to become children of God, to those who believe in His name" (John 1:12).

God created each one of us with a unique set of talents and traits that can be employed for His service as He wills. No person is without merit in His eyes. All are worthy of salvation. Furthermore, there is also no inherent goodness in any person that warrants salvation. No person has the prerogative to stand before God Almighty and say, "I deserve to be saved." Rather, we each must confess, "I *need* to be saved." As Paul declares, "For all have sinned and fall short of the glory of God" (Romans 3:23).

Developing a servant's heart is something that we do in *response* to God's gracious gifts of salvation, eternal life, and the Holy Spirit. It is never something that we do in order to *earn* salvation—to win, warrant, or put ourselves into a position to deserve it.

1. "The wages of sin is death, but the gift of God is eternal life in Christ Jesus our Lord" (Romans 6:23). What does Paul mean when he says the "wages of sin is death"?

2. Have you accepted God's offer of eternal life? If not, what is preventing you from accepting Christ as your Lord and Savior?

....

....

....

....

....

....

....

....

3. If so, what is your attitude toward serving others?

....

....

....

....

....

....

....

....

....

GOD'S PURPOSE FOR SAVING ME WAS TO BRING HIM GLORY

God saved us so that we might be His "trophies"—so that we might be examples to others of His love and mercy at work in and through a human life. Many people think that the reason for salvation is so they might go to heaven when they die. Although eternal life is certainly part of God's forgiveness plan for us, it is not the sole reason for our salvation. We are saved so that we might be *redeemed*. We once were in slavery to something that was evil, but we have been rescued and set free so that we might live a life of righteousness before God.

If God's only purpose for our salvation was so that we might go to heaven, He would be doing each of us a great favor by saving us and then immediately slaying us. Rather, His purpose for saving us is that we might reflect His nature. He wants us to represent Him on earth, doing the kinds of works that Jesus would do if He were walking in our shoes. God desires to manifest His character through our personalities and gifts. When we allow His Holy Spirit to work in and through us, we become vessels of His love in action. We reflect His compassion, love, and mercy to others. In so doing, we bring credit, honor, and glory to *Him*.

God does not save us so that we might be part of an elite group of "good people." He saves us so we might reach out to people with His goodness. He does not put us in the church so that we might soak up sermons, Bible conferences, prayer meetings, and seminars. He puts us in the church so that we might be of good use to those who are in need—so that we might function as His body, using our gifts, talents, and skills as the Holy Spirit directs us to help one another.

This is an important point for you to consider as you begin this Bible study. God did not save you simply so that you can have the assurance that you are going to heaven one day. He saved you in order that you might live every hour of every day of the remainder of your life in faithful service and obedience to Jesus Christ.

4. "But you are a chosen generation, a royal priesthood, a holy nation, His own special people" (1 Peter 2:9). What does it mean to be God's "trophy"?

5. What sort of a trophy has your life been in the past?

....

....

....

....

....

....

....

I AM MOST LIKE JESUS WHEN I SERVE OTHERS

The foremost characteristic of the life of Jesus Christ is *service*. We are most like Him when we serve as He served.

Many think that people are most like Jesus when they preach as Jesus preached, teach as Jesus taught, heal as Jesus healed, or perform miracles as Jesus performed miracles. They look only at the outward manifestation of people's witness and ministry. But we need to look beyond the outer manifestation to the motivation for Jesus' life: *service*. Jesus preached, taught, healed, and performed miracles to help others, not to call attention to Himself. He poured out His life so others might be saved, never thinking for a moment to save Himself. Time and again, Jesus said to those whom He had helped, "Don't tell anyone what has happened."

The critical point for you to recognize is that God has called you to serve others just as Jesus served them. He didn't save you or call you to service so that you might be exalted. He saved you so that you might serve others and bring praise and honor to His holy name. The good news is that any person who is saved *can* serve God and bring glory to Him. The nature of the ministry is not what is important—what *is* important is the motivation behind that service. God loved us so that we might love others. That is what the Christian life is all about.

6. In what ways do you presently serve other people? In what ways do you serve God?

_____

_____

_____

_____

_____

_____

_____

_____

_____

_____

7. How might God be calling you to serve others tomorrow?

_____

_____

_____

_____

_____

_____

_____

_____

_____

_____

DRAWING FROM THE TRUE SOURCE

At the outset of this study, I want to stress that we do not serve out of our *own* strength but out of the strength that Jesus provides. Let's face it . . . some people in our lives can be difficult to love. We all know people whom we would rather avoid than go out of our way to show love. Even more, serving can be difficult, time consuming, and draining. For this reason, we need to make sure we are connected to the right source before we seek to perform any act of service.

Hudson Taylor, a missionary to China, was a wonderful example of faith. What he accomplished in spreading the gospel of Christ has rarely been equaled in this age. But even he went through times when he was feeling worn out, sick, weary, and wanted to quit. One of his friends wrote him a letter and spoke to him about this need to draw his strength from Christ dwelling within him. All of a sudden, it dawned on Hudson that this was the answer. From that moment on, he began to serve the Lord not out of his own strength and energy but out of the power of the Holy Spirit that resided within him. God specializes in energizing the weak.

When the apostle Paul wrote, "we are more than conquerors through Him who loved us" (Romans 8:37), he was not expressing pride or egotism. He was not saying, "you name it, and we as believers can conquer it." Rather, his attitude was one of humility. Paul refused to boast about himself in any fashion or under any condition. As he said, "God forbid that I should boast except in the cross of our Lord Jesus Christ, by whom the world has been crucified to me, and I to the world" (Galatians 6:14). When Paul looked around, he could find nothing to boast about except one thing . . . and that was the cross.

Paul understand everything good that came his way happened because of the cross. The power of the cross had forever changed his life. As he wrote, "What things were gain to me, these I have counted loss for Christ. Yet indeed I also count all things loss for the excellence of the knowledge of Christ Jesus my Lord, for whom I have suffered the loss of all things, and count them as rubbish, that I may gain Christ and be found in Him" (Philippians 3:7–9). Furthermore, Paul realized what Hudson Taylor came to realize. All of his efforts for the gospel—no matter how noble—would fail if he were not drawing on Christ as his source.

As you begin this study on developing a servant's heart, make sure that you are tapping into the one true Source for your efforts. As you do, I am sure that you will find that "God shall supply all your need according to His riches in glory by Christ Jesus" (Philippians 4:19).

8. "Therefore I take pleasure in infirmities, in reproaches, in needs, in persecutions, in distresses, for Christ's sake. For when I am weak, then I am strong" (2 Corinthians 12:10). When have you found it to be true that when you were weak and weary, God provided a new reserve of strength to you?

9. What is an area of serving where you need to draw more on Christ's strength?

10. What hesitations do you have about serving others as you begin this study?

....

....

....

....

....

....

....

....

....

....

....

....

....

....

....

....

....

....

TODAY AND TOMORROW

Today: God wants His children to grow in service
to Him and to others.

Tomorrow: I will remember that I was saved to serve
and will look for opportunities to serve others.

CLOSING PRAYER

. . . .

Father, thank You for giving each of us talents, gifts, abilities, and resources. May we be the type of stewards who will not keep the gifts You provide for ourselves but use those resources to invest in eternity. Help us to minister freely to one another through our acts of service. We know that just attending church services is not enough—we want to actively engage in worshiping You by loving others. One day, when we stand before You on that final day, we want to hear You say to us, "Well done, my good and faithful servants."

Notes and Prayer Requests

Use this space to write any key points, questions, or prayer requests from this week's study.

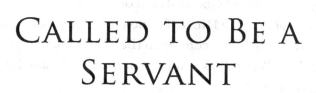

CALLED TO BE A SERVANT

IN THIS LESSON

Learning: What does it mean to be "planted like wheat" and "poured out like water"?

Growing: How can I learn to become a bondservant of Jesus Christ?

Jesus did not come into this world as a *superstar* but rather took on "the form of a bondservant" (Philippians 2:7). His three-year ministry was a powerful example of servanthood—from His first miracle of changing water to wine at a wedding feast to His sacrificial death on the cross, in which His own blood flowed freely for the salvation of all who would believe in Him and receive God's offer of forgiveness from sins. During His ministry, He made two great statements about servanthood that were references to His own life and sacrificial death: (1) *planted like wheat*, and (2) *poured out like water*. These statements from Jesus are also related to our roles as servants in God's kingdom today.

1. "Let this mind be in you which was also in Christ Jesus, who, being in the form of God, did not consider it robbery to be equal with God, but made Himself of no reputation, taking the form of a bondservant, and coming in the likeness of men" (Philippians 2:5–7). What does it mean that Christ "made Himself of no reputation"?

   ....

   ....

   ....

   ....

   ....

   ....

2. What does it mean to "let this mind be in you which was also in Christ Jesus"? What was Jesus' mindset? How does *your* mindset compare to that of Christ?

   ....

   ....

   ....

   ....

   ....

   ....

PLANTED LIKE WHEAT

Jesus spoke candidly with His disciples on several occasions about His impending death and resurrection. At the time, the disciples did not fully understand most of what Jesus was saying to them.

However, as they looked back and reflected on the time they had spent with Christ, they began to understand very clearly.

The disciple John recalled one incident in particular that occurred just before Passover. Jesus had just raised Lazarus from the dead in the nearby town of Bethany, and the news of this event had spread quickly and widely. Many people had lined the path leading into Jerusalem from the Mount of Olives to welcome Jesus as their king. "The next day a great multitude that had come to the feast, when they heard that Jesus was coming to Jerusalem, took branches of palm trees and went out to meet Him, and cried out: 'Hosanna! "Blessed is He who comes in the name of the LORD!" The King of Israel!'" (John 12:12–13).

Jesus was being pressured to make a public move to consolidate power and become an earthly ruler in place of the Romans and the legalistic Jewish leaders. Sometime later, John relates how a group of Greeks—who had come to Jerusalem to worship at the feast—asked to have a private audience with Jesus. "Now there were certain Greeks among those who came up to worship at the feast. Then they came to Philip, who was from Bethsaida of Galilee, and asked him, saying, 'Sir, we wish to see Jesus.' Philip came and told Andrew, and in turn Andrew and Philip told Jesus" (verses 20–22).

From a human perspective, this could have become a top-level meeting that led to a human-engineered political coup. In fact, when Jesus was approached with the invitation, He replied to Philip, "The hour has come that the Son of Man should be glorified" (verse 23). On the surface, the disciples might have taken this be a strong statement that Jesus was indicating *now was the time* for Him to assume political authority. After all, to be *glorified* means to reach one's crowning moment and shining hour. But then Jesus quickly went on to say, "Most assuredly, I say to you, unless a grain of wheat falls into the ground and dies, it remains alone; but if it dies, it produces much grain. He who loves his life will lose it, and he who hates his life in this world will keep it for eternal life" (verses 24–25).

Jesus made it clear that God had not called Him to be a political king so that people might experience a better earthly existence. Rather, His heavenly Father had sent Him to earth to die a sacrificial death so that people might experience eternal life. Jesus' higher and more meaningful goal was not to be achieved by human-made systems and alliances of this world, but through the ultimate act of ministry and servanthood—a sacrificial death.

Jesus followed His statement to Philip and Andrew by saying, "If anyone serves Me, let him follow Me; and where I am, there My servant will be also. If anyone serves Me, him My Father will honor" (verse 26). Jesus chose the servant role for Himself—which was actually the heavenly Father's role for Him. He then called His followers to become like Him and to be, first and foremost, *servants*. Jesus concluded, "What shall I say? 'Father, save Me from this hour'? But for this purpose I came to this hour. Father, glorify Your name" (verses 27–28).

Jesus did not back away from servanthood or the ultimate act of service—His sacrificial death. He did not regard His crucifixion in any way to be a demeaning or diminishing act but considered it to be the very purpose for His life and the fulfillment of His time on this earth. His entire life and ministry had led up to this supreme act of service.

3. Jesus lived a life of service and died a death that was an act of service. What new insights do you have into the way that Jesus was a servant?

4. Think of one or two people who have served you in a Christlike way. What did they do that was meaningful? How did they affect your life?

....

....

....

....

....

....

....

POURED OUT LIKE WATER

David wrote a prophetic psalm that is closely linked to the crucifixion of Jesus. He begins by saying, "My God, My God, why have You forsaken Me?" (Psalm 22:1)—a phrase that Jesus would echo from on the cross (see Matthew 27:46). David continues, "I am poured out like water, and all My bones are out of joint; my heart is like wax; it has melted within Me" (verse 14).

The very life essence of Jesus was "poured out like water." During His ministry, He poured Himself out on all those who were hungry and thirsty for the things of God (see John 6:35). He gave of Himself freely to all who came to Him in need. He said to a woman by a well in Samaria, "Whoever drinks of the water that I shall give him will never thirst. But the water that I shall give him will become in him a fountain of water springing up into everlasting life" (John 4:14). During His crucifixion, blood and water mingled freely, flowing from Jesus' side (see John 19:34). He willingly gave His life . . . His blood "poured out" for the sins of the world.

The purpose of being *planted* like a grain of wheat or *poured out* like water is not the sacrificial giving itself but what follows such service: a great blessing and reward. When a grain of wheat is planted, the seed dies, but it brings an abundant harvest. The single dying grain produces "much grain" (John 12:24). In pouring Himself out, Jesus intended that His own spirit become a "fountain of water springing up" (John 4:14).

Death or sacrifice in itself is not the goal. Being a servant does not mean that we have a martyr's complex—a desire to die just for the sake of dying. Rather, our lives are to be poured out in loving service so that what we give to others bears the quality of life within it. In pouring ourselves out to others, others can experience greater life, and we experience a more purposeful life. The end result is not a moot death but a glorious and everlasting abundance.

Jesus called His disciples (including you and me) to follow Him in servanthood because it brings about a great blessings. Among the many benefits of servanthood are: (1) an excitement for God and for all things that are good, (2) a healing in our lives, (3) a difference in the lives of those we serve, (4) inspiration and motivation to those who benefit from and who witness our generous service, and (5) a more fruitful life—both in the natural and supernatural realms.

5. "Most assuredly, I say to you, unless a grain of wheat falls into the ground and dies, it remains alone; but if it dies, it produces much grain. He who loves his life will lose it, and he who hates his life in this world will keep it for eternal life. If anyone serves Me, let him follow Me; and where I am, there My servant will be also. If anyone serves Me, him My Father will honor" (John 12:24-26). What do Jesus' words in this passage teach you about the cost of being a servant?

6. What do you learn about the rewards of service from Jesus' words?

....

....

....

....

....

....

....

....

....

BONDSERVANTS FOR CHRIST

Jesus' disciples and early followers had a clear understanding of their role as servants. This is evident from the way they later described themselves in their letters to other believers. Peter described himself as "a bondservant and apostle of Jesus Christ" (2 Peter 1:1). James wrote that he was "a bondservant of God and of the Lord Jesus Christ" (James 1:1). Paul likewise described himself as "a bondservant of Jesus Christ, called to be an apostle" (Romans 1:1).

The Greek word that is generally translated as *bondservant* in the New Testament is a term that was also used at the time to refer to the "lower rowers"—the galley slaves who were kept in chains below the decks of large ships. These slaves did the exhausting, difficult, and unseen work of rowing vessels across the seas and through the storms.

There is nothing about this image that compels others to praise and admire such a servant . . . for the work that he or she does goes mostly unrecognized and unrewarded by others. Yet this is the word the disciples and the early followers of Christ chose to describe themselves in their work for the gospel. They saw it as an honor to be a bondservant of Christ Jesus—a "lower rower" in the work of God's kingdom.

This concept of success is completely inverted from the world's standard. The world tells us that a successful person is the one who is at the top—the one who is the most visible and most accomplished. However, the Bible tells us that in God's eyes, the successful person is the one who is willing to be a lower rower for the benefit of others and for the sake of the gospel.

The disciples and followers of Christ recognized the blessing that came from being a bondservant. They knew their efforts in the spiritual realm were cause for joy, because they were helping others to find eternal life in Christ Jesus. As Paul wrote to the believers in Philippi from a jail cell, "If I am being poured out as a drink offering on the sacrifice and service of your faith, I am glad and rejoice with you all" (Philippians 2:17).

The disciples fully embraced their role. They knew it was their calling and identity, *not because they were leaders of the church,* but because they were following in the steps of Jesus Christ, the first and foremost Servant of God. We are likewise called to be servants and to have the heart of a servant as our hallmark. Servanthood is to be our attitude and our motivation as we follow Christ Jesus our Lord.

7. How do you imagine it would feel to be a "lower rower" on a ship in the first century? How does it feel at times to be a "lower rower" in the kingdom of God?

8. What are a few things that you would consider "lower rower" positions of service? Why are they so unattractive to you?

....

....

....

....

....

....

....

....

....

....

ALL ARE CALLED TO SERVE

Some believers feel that it is only the pastors or other members of a church staff who are God's servants. In reality, *any person* who has accepted Jesus Christ as Savior is called to be a servant of God. We are *all* called to be God's ministers to others in particular areas of need, and at particular times, but *always* with a mind and a heart motivated toward generous service.

No one is excluded from such service. We have each been commissioned by God to serve Him and to serve others in need every day of our lives. As the apostle Paul writes, "For by grace you have been saved through faith, and that not of yourselves; it is the gift of God, not of works, lest anyone should boast. For we are His workmanship, created in Christ Jesus for good works, which God prepared beforehand that we should walk in them" (Ephesians 2:8–10).

Service is an act of *doing* of good works *as God leads and directs* through the power of the Holy Spirit. The works are there for us to do. Our responsibility is to obey God—even as Jesus obeyed His heavenly Father—and serve Him with *all* of our lives. We are to offer up every last "grain" and "pour out" every bit of our lives to Him and others.

9. What does it mean to be God's *workmanship*? How do you reconcile the fact that you were "created in Christ Jesus for good works" with the fact that your salvation is by faith alone and is not based on any good works on your part?

....

....

....

....

....

....

....

10. How is the Lord challenging you to reevaluate your concept of service? In what ways is the Lord challenging you to engage in more active servanthood?

....

....

....

....

....

....

....

TODAY AND TOMORROW

Today: Jesus and His disciples set the example for me of becoming a bondservant of Christ.

Tomorrow: I will not run away from opportunities to serve, even if it means being a "lower rower."

CLOSING PRAYER

Lord, when You call us to serve others, we never want to say no to You—whether we voice it in words or live it out through our inaction. We want to be the kind of people who, when people look back on our lives, will say that we made a difference for You. We want to be planted like wheat and poured out like water for Your kingdom. Help us to come to grips with what You require of us when it comes to loving and serving others. Let us be the type of people who can honestly say, "Lord, here we are, send us to do whatever You desire for as long as it takes."

NOTES AND PRAYER REQUESTS

Use this space to write any key points, questions, or prayer requests from this week's study.

A SERVANT'S SPIRIT

IN THIS LESSON

Learning: What are the three marks of
a true servant?

Growing: How can I learn to serve
without expecting any reward?

The world has a hierarchy, a "ladder," for evaluating the success of a person. Sometimes that ladder is based on fame, and sometimes it is based on money. Those who have made their way to the position of chief executive officer are considered at the top of the ladder.

This is not new to our century. Jesus often had to deal with this concern about position and authority throughout His ministry. In fact, He had to deal with this thinking even among His *own disciples.* During the Last Supper, Luke records that a dispute arose among the disciples "as to which of them should be considered the greatest"

(Luke 22:24). Jesus had to say to them, "The kings of the Gentiles exercise lordship over them, and those who exercise authority over them are called 'benefactors.' But not so among you; on the contrary, he who is greatest among you, let him be as the younger, and he who governs as he who serves" (verses 25–26).

The concept must have seemed upside down to the disciples—that service should equal greatness. It was a perspective that went against the grain, against common sense, and against the prevailing world opinion. It still does. Today, if people engage in servanthood all the time, they are considered to be wimps, chumps, or doormats.

Those who are widely admired by the masses tend to be the people who have shown themselves to have the most power, the most appeal, the most intelligence, the most money, and the most accomplishment—the one at the top of the scale. But God does not deal in hierarchies . . . only in categories. A person is either saved or unsaved. A person is either following God in obedience or is rebelling. A person is either a servant or not a servant.

A SIMPLE DEFINITION

Jesus gave a simple definition of service when He said, "He who loves his life will lose it, and he who hates his life in this world will keep it for eternal life" (John 12:25). Those who love their lives are the ones who are self-centered, selfish, and greedy—those who live totally for their own benefit. These are the people who desire to be *served*. In the end, they will lose everything they have ever attempted to gain. On the other hand, those who "hate" their lives are the ones who are willing to put others first—those who give and help others. These are the individuals who are *servants*. In the end, Jesus said, they will enter into eternal life.

Some people confuse "hating one's life" with having low self-esteem or with diminishing their gifts. We are to value ourselves highly. We are to recognize we are wonderful and unique creations of God. Each of us has been given a set of gifts, traits, and talents by God. We have been designed with a specific purpose in mind—we *are* God's workmanship (see Ephesians 2:10). We are God's treasure, His delight, His chosen vessels, and His beloved children. In truth, God valued us so highly that He sent His Son, Jesus Christ, to die on the cross so we might be reconciled to God and live with Him forever. God's love alone gives our lives great value!

In recognizing our great value to God, we have a servant's spirit when we are willing to *use* our gifts for the benefit of others and not solely to bring applause, recognition, or reward to ourselves. We "hate ourselves," from God's standpoint, when we completely abandon our own self-advancement in order to help others or to fulfill whatever call God has placed on our lives.

What often tends to happen is that those who love their lives tend to hate the lives of other people. They use, abuse, and manipulate others for their own goals and purposes. But those who "hate" their lives are those who choose to love others more than they love their own advancement. They bless others, give to them, and benefit them.

This is the quality of life that Jesus lived. He didn't dislike Himself or hate the call of God on His life. He knew who He was—and He fully embraced what His heavenly Father had commanded Him to be and to do. But He didn't exalt Himself, seek His own fame and power, or attract attention to Himself. His purpose was to bring glory to the Father and to obey the Father in all things. His purpose was to *serve*.

Jesus taught, "To whom much is given, from him much will be required" (Luke 12:48). The more we recognize all that God has given to us—including His greatest gift to us, our salvation—the more we should recognize that we are required to give much in the way of service. Those who have the greater talents are required to give the greater service.

When Paul wrote that Jesus emptied Himself of His heavenly identity and became a bondservant of God (see Philippians 2:5–7), he was not implying that Jesus was unworthy or undeserving of a good reputation. Jesus had the ultimate reputation in that He never sinned against God or man—but He didn't concern Himself with the world's opinion. Some people "work themselves to death" to get ahead in life, but Jesus "gave Himself to death." Those who follow His example and give themselves to death receive the great rewards in eternity.

1. What does it mean that Jesus "gave Himself to death"? How might you imitate that attitude this week?

....

....

....

....

....

....

....

....

....

2. What things has God given you that He wants you to share with others? (Consider your time, money, talents, and so forth.)

....

....

....

....

....

....

....

....

....

....

SERVANTS DO NOT DEMAND RECOGNITION

Those who have the genuine heart of a servant will possess three main attributes. *First, they will not demand recognition.* Servants are willing to remain in the shadows or the "lower galleys." They give without acknowledgment—in fact, they are willing to give so that no one else knows who has done the giving! Jesus said that God honors such acts of service done in private and rewards such individuals openly (see Matthew 6:3-4).

However, the same is not true of those who seek the praise of other people. As Jesus warned, "Take heed that you do not do your charitable deeds before men, to be seen by them. Otherwise you have no reward from your Father in heaven. Therefore, when you do a charitable deed, do not sound a trumpet before you as the hypocrites do in the synagogues and in the streets, that they may have glory from men. Assuredly, I say to you, they have their reward" (verses 1-2).

The reward received by those who seek praise from people is just that and only that—praise from *people*. Such praise comes and goes quickly, for the approval of people is fickle and often fleeting. God's praise and blessing, on the other hand, are reserved for those who serve others without any expectation of recognition or praise from people.

I am continually amazed at how many people in the body of Christ only want to participate in various aspects of their churches if their names are listed on the committee roster, published in the service bulletin, or engraved somewhere on a plaque. I was even once told by a development officer for an organization that fewer projects are named in *honor* of major contributors—the prevailing practice is now to *include* the naming of a building, hospital wing, or park as a part of the negotiating process for securing the donation in the first place. As Jesus said, those who desire public acclaim have their reward—but it is not an eternal reward.

3. How do you feel when you don't receive recognition for something that you have done?

....

....

....

....

....

4. When have you performed some "selfless act" that was secretly motivated by a desire for recognition?

....

....

....

....

....

....

SERVANTS DO NOT DEMAND REWARDS

Second, true servants do not demand rewards. Servants give without expecting anything in return from those whom they serve. True servanthood is void of manipulation or a desire to control others. In the ancient world, the best thing that could happen to a slave or a servant was to have a benevolent master. Servants in such households knew all their needs would be met. Such servants had a sense of security and safety. They were not merely the property of the master or "lord" but were considered valuable assets to be nurtured and rewarded.

Abraham was such a master. In Genesis 24:2, we read that his oldest servant "ruled over all that he had," and Abraham entrusted him to travel a great distance by himself to find a wife for his son, Isaac. This servant was faithful to his duty. He had no thought of escaping to "freedom" with Abraham's ten camels and the considerable wealth entrusted to him. Likewise, Joseph was a favored servant in the household of the Egyptian Potiphar, who "left all that he had in Joseph's hand" (Genesis 39:6).

Our role as a bondservant of Christ is of a similar nature. Jesus Christ is our *Lord*. He is our Master, our Ruler, our Owner. He is the One who has redeemed our lives from death. He is the One from whom we take our daily orders and from whom we receive all that we need. He is the One who has entrusted us to conduct spiritual business in His name. Genuine servants know they have all they need in Christ Jesus—all that is truly important, desirable, and of value. When we give, we *will* receive. But what comes back to us will be from God's hand and at God's command. We are to expect to receive from God *not* because we have given but because God is faithful in providing for His children, often through supernatural means.

Expecting God to provide for us out of His great storehouse of blessing is far different from *demanding* that God provide for us or reward us because of what we have done. Expecting from God is a mark of faith. Demanding God to act is a mark of pride.

5. "Do not seek what you should eat or what you should drink, nor have an anxious mind. For all these things the nations of the world seek after, and your Father knows that you need these things" (Luke 12:29-30). What does it mean to have "an anxious mind"? How can an anxious mind affect your service to others and to the Lord?

6. If you truly do not worry about what you will eat for our next meal, how might that affect your service to others? How can you gain that attitude?

....

....

....

....

....

....

....

SERVANTS DO NOT DEMAND SELF-RIGHTS

Finally, true servants do not demand self-rights. Servants have a "yielded" spirit, both to God and to others. They will stand up for what is right in God's eyes but will not insist that they have to have their own way. Servants "yield the right of way" to others, or as Paul wrote, "[give] preference to one another" (Romans 12:10).

The hallmark of the Christian life is as follows: "Giving thanks always for all things to God the Father in the name of our Lord Jesus Christ, submitting to one another in the fear of God" (Ephesians 5:20–21). We are to love God with all of our heart, soul, and mind, and our neighbors as ourselves. It is out of love we serve. In fact, service is the manifestation of love. If we love but do not give to others and are not generous in our service, on what grounds can we truly say that we love? Service is the *evidence* of genuine love. It is love in action.

7. "Jesus said to him, "'you shall love the LORD your God with all your heart, with all your soul, and with all your mind.' This is the first and great commandment. And the second is like it: 'you shall love your neighbor as yourself'" (Matthew 22:37-39). Notice that Jesus does *not* say, "you shall learn to love yourself in order

to love others." What does this suggest about our culture's emphasis on self-esteem and self-love?

8. In what way is the second command ("love your neighbor") like the first command ("love the LORD your God")? How are the two commands dependent on each another?

A Serious Challenge

If most of us were asked whether we were God's servants, we would likely respond, "Yes, I am. He is my King, and I am His subject." However, the more difficult questions to answer are these: "Do we truly have a servant's heart? Are we willing to serve? Are we presently serving others without demanding recognition, rewards, or rights?"

Many people only give lip service to servanthood. They say they are servants, want to be servants, or wish they were better servants. The truth is that we can all grow in our desire, ability, and effectiveness as servants. However, we must actually *be* servants—not just talk about being servants.

As James said, "Be doers of the word, and not hearers only, deceiving yourselves. For if anyone is a hearer of the word and not a doer, he is like a man observing his natural face in a mirror; for he observes himself, goes away, and immediately forgets what kind of man he was. But he who looks into the perfect law of liberty and continues in it, and is not a forgetful hearer but a doer of the work, this one will be blessed in what he does" (James 1:22–25). The true servant is one who has a heart for service . . . the one who is actually engaged in serving.

9. "When you do a charitable deed, do not let your left hand know what your right hand is doing, that your charitable deed may be in secret; and your Father who sees in secret will Himself reward you openly" (Matthew 6:3–4). What does it mean to "not let your left hand know what your right hand is doing"? When have you seen God publicly rewarding you for charitable deeds that you have done in private?

....

....

....

....

....

....

....

....

10. "And if you do good to those who do good to you, what credit is that to you? For even sinners do the same. And if you lend to those from whom you hope to receive back, what credit is that to you? For even sinners lend to sinners to receive as much back. But love your enemies, do good, and lend, hoping for nothing in return; and your reward will be great, and you will be sons of the Most High. For He is kind to the unthankful and evil" (Luke

6:33-35). How do we balance the command to love our enemies with the need to stand firm against evil? Where does service to others fit into this balance?

TODAY AND TOMORROW

Today: The three marks of a true servant are not demanding recognition, reward, or rights.

Tomorrow: I will prayerfully work on serving others without demanding anything in return.

CLOSING PRAYER

Heavenly Father, fasten this message into our hearts and help us to continually seek to exhibit the three marks of a genuine servant. Help us to refuse the urge to demand recognition for our deeds. Help us to look only to You for our rewards and not chase after the affirmation of others. Help us to serve You wholeheartedly and not insist on our own rights. Grant us wisdom today to discover our gifts and realize that we cannot justify refusing to use our talents to serve You.

NOTES AND PRAYER REQUESTS

Use this space to write any key points, questions, or prayer requests from this week's study.

JESUS: OUR ROLE MODEL AS SERVANT

IN THIS LESSON

Learning: What kinds of people did Jesus serve?

Growing: What should be my attitude when serving unpleasant people?

One of the names given to Jesus in the New Testament is "Son of David." For many people, this title evokes the kingship of Jesus—and rightfully so. David was a great king, and Jesus is our King of kings. However, the apostle Paul states that "David . . . served his own generation by the will of God" (Acts 13:36). The first disciples of Jesus did not regard David as a great soldier, statesman, king, or psalmist, but as a *servant*. They perceived David as being used by God for God's purposes. David functioned as a servant of God to the people of Israel. David's most important trait was servanthood under God's command and authority.

In this way, Jesus is most assuredly like David. He was and is the supreme servant. Both David and Jesus knew the secret for true success from God's perspective: *Discover God's goals for your life and then achieve those goals.* God's goals for David were that he unify God's people into one nation, create a centralized place for worship, place a renewed emphasis on praise before God, and defeat the enemies of God. In fulfilling these goals, David *served* the Lord.

God's goal in sending Jesus to this earth was that He might show us what God is like, through both word and deed, revealing to us a loving, healing, saving, and delivering heavenly Father. God's goal was also that Jesus might become the definitive and universal sacrifice for the sins of all mankind. In fulfilling these goals, Jesus *served* the Lord.

A Life of Service

We often think of Jesus' ministry, or His years of "active service," as being the final three years of His life. What we often fail to recognize is that for nearly thirty years, Jesus *served* His family. The historical tradition within the church is that Joseph, Jesus' earthly father, died when Jesus was a young man, perhaps even a young teenager. As the eldest son in the family, Jesus became responsible for the general well-being of His mother and His earthly brothers and sisters. In all likelihood, Jesus filled this role in a practical way—providing the family income and helping in the training of his younger siblings.

It was in serving His family that Jesus developed a great deal of the compassion that we see in Him during His ministry years. He reached out to children, He touched lepers, and He embraced outcasts. Compassion is a trait that is part of Jesus' *humanity* as much as His divinity. This ability to care for others is not an ability that one can develop overnight. Rather, it was a pattern that Jesus developed throughout His years of caring for His family.

1. How do you feel about the service that you give your family? How do you feel it compares with the way that Jesus cared for His family?

2. What goals do you believe God has for you? How is fulfilling those goals your means of serving God?

A PROFOUND ACT OF SERVICE

One of the most profound acts of service in Jesus' life occurred during the Last Supper. John writes, "[Jesus] rose from supper and laid aside His garments, took a towel and girded Himself. After that, He poured water into a basin and began to wash the disciples' feet, and to wipe them with the towel with which He was girded. . . . He said to them, 'Do you know what I have done to you? You call Me Teacher and Lord, and you say well, for so I am. If I then, your Lord and Teacher, have washed your feet, you also ought to wash one another's feet. For I have given you an example, that you should do as I have done to you. Most assuredly, I say to you, a servant is not greater than his master; nor is he who is sent greater than he who sent him. If you know these things, blessed are you if you do them'" (John 13:4–5, 12–17).

Jesus, in performing the act of washing the disciples' feet, was most concerned that they saw His attitude and character of ministry. He used this vivid means of demonstration so His disciples would never forget this principal truth: *you must be the servants of one another.* As previously mentioned, we also know from Luke's account that the disciples were debating during the Last Supper as to which of them was to be considered the greatest (see Luke 22:24). Jesus' response to this dispute was to perform an act of service.

Normally, the host would provide servants to wash the feet of guests as they entered the house. Guests were expected to come to banquets having bathed and wearing clean garments. This is what Jesus meant, in part, when He said, "He who is bathed needs only to wash his feet, but is completely clean; and you are clean" (John 13:10). Yet His meaning went deeper, for Jesus was referring to the disciples' spiritual nature. He explained, "You are already clean because of the word which I have spoken to you. Abide in Me, and I in you" (John 15:3–4). Jesus knew all but one of His disciples had fully believed His words and were abiding in Him. (Only Judas had chosen to harbor rebellion in his heart and was *not* abiding in Christ).

Peter was sitting at the "foot" of the table, which might account for opposition to Jesus washing his feet. In occupying that position, it was Peter's responsibility to be the servant of the table. If feet needed washing, it should have been Peter who was doing the washing. He may have felt embarrassed that Jesus was preparing to do what he should have done. Yet Jesus insisted on washing Peter's feet. He wanted Peter to learn that unless he received all that Jesus desired to do for him, he would not be in a position to serve others.

The lesson to Peter and the other disciples was this: *As Jesus served them, so they were to serve others.* They were to be just as sensitive as Jesus to the needs of others and just as generous as Jesus in their loving care of others. The same is true for us. We are to serve others in humility and kindness, just as Jesus washed the dusty feet of His disciples.

3. "Most assuredly, I say to you, a servant is not greater than his master; nor is he who is sent greater than he who sent him. If you know these things, blessed are you if you do them" (John 13:16–17). According to Jesus, what are you really saying if you consider yourself to be above certain types of service?

4. What types of blessings might God bestow on you if you have a true servant's heart?

SERVICE TO THE LEAST DESERVING

It is important to note that Jesus washed the feet of Judas. He knelt before the man who would betray Him within a matter of hours in the Garden of Gethsemane. Jesus *knew* what He was doing even as He washed the feet of Judas. He said, "I know whom I have chosen" (John 13:18).

Most of us find it easy to serve those we consider "good" people. It is much more difficult to serve those whom we consider "bad." It is much harder to take a basin and towel and to kneel before a mean-spirited, deliberately rebellious, or hardened person. However, we must follow the example of Jesus. He washed the feet of the man who represented the ultimate hypocrite—one who was pleasant to His face but opposed Him in his heart.

Paul had specific words to say to those who found it difficult to serve their masters (see Ephesians 6:5–6). Some members of the first-century church were slaves—some to Christian masters and some to unbelievers. These slaves, free in their spirits in Christ Jesus, nonetheless were called to continue to be servants. These believers were richly blessed and endowed with spiritual gifts, yet they were required to continue to do the most humbling acts of service.

5. When have you been required to serve someone who was unlovable or difficult to please? How did you feel about your service?

6. When have you been served by someone, even though you knew that you were not being Christlike yourself? How did you feel about that person's service to you?

Serving "As Unto the Lord"

Jesus was engaging in one of the most menial household tasks when He set about washing each of His disciples' feet. In doing so, He was sending a clear message that He was willing to do *anything* for them. The disciples learned the lesson. From the time of Jesus' resurrection onward, they equated all forms of service as a means of serving Jesus . . . regardless of how humbling or menial that act of service seemed.

Jesus had taught them this lesson by washing their feet—and by receiving a special gift from Mary of Bethany. John writes, "Six days before the Passover, Jesus came to Bethany, where Lazarus was who had been dead, whom He had raised from the dead. There they made Him a supper; and Martha served, but Lazarus was one of those who sat at the table with Him. Then Mary took a pound of very costly oil of spikenard, anointed the feet of Jesus, and wiped His feet with her hair. And the house was filled with the fragrance of the oil" (John 12:1–3).

Judas objected to the gift, saying, "Why was this fragrant oil not sold for three hundred denarii and given to the poor" (verse 5). But Jesus replied, "Let her alone; she has kept this for the day of My burial" (verse 7). Jesus knew how to serve His disciples by washing their feet, but He also knew how to *receive* the service of those who loved and followed Him. He allowed Mary to anoint His feet and to demonstrate her love in this way.

When we serve others, we ultimately are serving Jesus. We are demonstrating our love for Him in the way that we minister to others. Our service to others is also a sign of Jesus' resurrection power and His desire to save and heal all humankind. Our service—whatever we do to promote the kingdom of God—is the greatest witness that we can give to the Lord Jesus.

So, are you willing to do *anything* that God asks of you today? God will never ask you to do anything that is sinful or foolish—but He may ask you to do something menial. I have never had a person come to me and say, "Pastor, give me the most menial job in the church. Give me the chore that is the worst to do or the job that is least likely to be recognized." If such a person had come to me, I certainly would have felt that I was in the presence of genuine greatness!

If you are too good for a task, the reality is that you probably are not good enough for it in God's eyes. Any job done "as unto the Lord" is a worthy one, regardless of the nature of the job or the degree of recognition. Is there anybody whose feet you would refuse to wash? That may very well be the person whom God most wants you to serve!

7. "He who is greatest among you shall be your servant" (Matthew 23:11). How does this "hierarchy of greatness" compare with what you find in the world—at work, school, in politics, and elsewhere? How much does your life reflect this attitude?

8. "The kingdom of God is not eating and drinking, but righteousness and peace and joy in the Holy Spirit. For he who serves Christ in these things is acceptable to God and approved by men" (Romans 14:17–18). How are "peace and joy" acts of service? What does this principle teach about what your attitude should be toward service?

THE GREATEST SERVICE OF ALL

Jesus' ultimate act of service can be summed up in one word: *cross*. As I indicated at the outset of this lesson, God's goal for Jesus was that He become the sacrifice for our sin. Jesus fulfilled that goal in His death on the cross.

God doesn't let any person get away with sin. Sin causes us to be estranged from Him, and His purpose is always to bring us to reconciliation with Himself. He continues to convict us of our sin until we come to a point of confession. If we fall into sin and error, the Holy Spirit convicts us until we confess and, by His power, repent and live in righteousness before Him.

The soul that sins willfully and continually ultimately dies (see Acts 3:23). Jesus was God's supreme means of atonement—of bringing God and humans into relationship so that we might be free of guilt and eternal death. It is for this purpose of atonement that Jesus came into the world.

A significant part of God's purpose for your life is that you be a witness to God's love through all that you do and say. You are to be a witness to God's saving power. You are not required by God to die on the cross, but you are called by God to live and die in such a way that others are made increasingly aware of God's plan of forgiveness for them.

Service cannot be separated from witness or ministry. When you serve others with joy, peace, and righteousness radiating from you, you are a witness to God's love and desire to forgive, a witness to Christ's crucifixion and resurrection, and a witness to the Holy Spirit's empowering and guiding presence. When you serve others, you *are* a minister—you are embodying the work of the Holy Spirit to others.

Without a servant's heart, you may give a *form* of witness or ministry, but you will not be a genuine witness, and your ministry will not bear much fruit. We must have a servant's heart and be motivated by our love for Christ Jesus.

9. "He said to them, 'Whoever desires to come after Me, let him deny himself, and take up his cross, and follow Me'" (Mark 8:34). What does it mean to deny ourselves? What does it mean to take up our crosses? How do we do this in everyday life?

10. "Then Jesus . . . said, 'Assuredly, I say to you, unless you are converted and become as little children, you will by no means enter the kingdom of heaven'" (Matthew 18:2–3). What does it mean to "become as little children"? Why does Jesus say that we cannot enter the kingdom of heaven unless we become like children?

TODAY AND TOMORROW

Today: Jesus spent His life serving everyone that He met, no matter how unpleasant.

Tomorrow: I will prayerfully strive to serve everyone that I meet—even those whom I don't like.

CLOSING PRAYER

Jesus, You lived a lifetime of service. You washed all of the disciples' feet at the Last Supper—including the feet of the one who would betray You. Help us today to follow Your example and serve others regardless of our feelings toward them. We know that a true servant of Your kingdom does not choose the ones to serve . . . we just obediently follow Your call to serve as You lead us. Let us be humble in spirit. Let us never think too highly of ourselves. Rather, let us be willing to reach down and perform the lowest acts of service, just as You did on earth.

NOTES AND PRAYER REQUESTS

Use this space to write any key points, questions, or prayer requests from this week's study.

THE PATTERN FOR SERVICE

IN THIS LESSON

Learning: What are the steps of service
in day-to-day terms?

Growing: How can I make service the
central habit of my life?

The service that Jesus performed during His ministry almost always follows a specific sequence. A prime example is found in Jesus' interactions with Zacchaeus, a tax collector who lived in Jericho. Jesus was on His way to Jerusalem for the final time—probably less than two weeks away from His death—when he met the tax collector. As Luke relates, Zacchaeus was of "short stature," so he climbed a sycamore tree to better see Jesus. Luke tells us what happened next:

When Jesus came to the place, He looked up and saw him, and said to him, "Zacchaeus, make haste and come down, for today I must stay at your house." So he made haste and came down, and received Him joyfully. But when [the crowd] saw it they all complained, saying, "He has gone to be a guest with a man who is a sinner."

Then Zacchaeus stood and said to the Lord, "Look, Lord, I give half of my goods to the poor; and if I have taken anything from anyone by false accusation, I restore fourfold."

And Jesus said to him, "Today salvation has come to this house, because he also is a son of Abraham; for the Son of Man has come to seek and to save that which was lost" (Luke 19:5–10).

The sequence of service is fivefold: (1) awareness, (2) availability, (3) acceptance, (4) abiding, and (5) abandonment. In this lesson, we will look at each of these steps.

AWARENESS AND AVAILABILITY

The first step is awareness. Zacchaeus was a wealthy, hopeful, yet desperate man. Luke tells us that he was short in stature, which explains why he climbed up into a sycamore tree. But Jesus did not single out Zacchaeus because he was short or because he was in a tree. Jesus responded to Zacchaeus because He saw in him a need, a desire, and a longing.

Zacchaeus was the chief tax collector in Jericho and worked for Rome. He was considered by his fellow Jews to be part of the evil oppression that had been placed on the Jewish people by the Roman occupation forces. Tax collectors working for Rome often collected more than what was due, and they became wealthy in the process of cheating others. Tax collectors were much despised and considered to be great sinners.

John said that Jesus "knew all men, and had no need that anyone should testify of man, for He knew what was in man" (John 2:24–25). We find evidence of this a number of times in the Gospels when we read of how Jesus knew the hearts of people or how He knew what people were thinking and trying to do. Jesus *knew* Zacchaeus, even though they had never met. He saw him as a man desperate for God's grace, not as a man who cheated on collecting taxes.

If we do not see people as Jesus saw them, we cannot minister as Jesus did. Before we can reach out to help someone, we must first see that person as having a need. Many people are so totally turned inward that they don't see others or hear their inner moaning and weeping. We all have problems, worries, temptations, and sorrows that nobody knows about.

We are called to become so sensitive to the needs of others that we *know* when they are in need of healing and are reaching out to Jesus—even though they may not initially confess their need. We are to serve those in need with confidence and with confidentiality. Our service to them can cause them to touch Jesus with renewed faith and bring them healing.

The second step in the process of serving is availability. Jesus was never too busy to respond to those who sought out His help. When Jesus encountered Zacchaeus, He was on His way to a final week of ministry in the city of Jerusalem—a week that would ultimately culminate in His death on the cross and His resurrection. Nothing was more important than this event. Yet Jesus had *time* for Zacchaeus, even though he was a hated tax collector, sinner, and an outcast in the eyes of all who lived in Jericho. Jesus made Himself available to Zacchaeus and had time for him.

People today are starving for the gifts of time and concern. They are desperate for someone to listen to them and pay attention to them. Sometimes, those who need our time and attention the most are those who are held in low esteem by society. Prisons, nursing homes, and hospitals are filled with people who are lonely and forsaken.

1. Think of a time when you discovered that someone was much different on the inside than you originally expected. What was your reaction when you discovered the "real person" inside? What had made you expect something different?

2. When have you been surprised in the past to learn that people misunderstood who you really were? What made them expect something different?

3. "Let no one seek his own, but each one the other's well-being" (1 Corinthians 10:24). Think back over the past week. When did you have opportunities to set aside your own wellbeing in order to serve someone else? What did you do?

ACCEPTANCE AND ABIDING

The third step in the process of serving is acceptance. Notice that Jesus did not say to Zacchaeus, "Clean up your act. When you stop collecting taxes, I will come to your house." He accepted Zacchaeus just as he was.

Of course, accepting others does not mean that we accept the way they are without intending to help them change things for the better. Rather, it means accepting them the way that they are so that we might help them move forward in their lives. In the story told in the Gospel of Luke, Jesus did not leave Zacchaeus the same way that He found him. Zacchaeus had a change of heart as a result of Jesus going to his house.

Our motivation must always be to serve people in Christ so they can become all they can be as God's children. Acceptance is neither a denial of their current condition nor a belief that things can never improve for them. We err greatly if we require others to "get good" before we help them "get God." God did not place any preconditions on us before He forgave us generously. We are therefore in no position to place conditions on others. We must accept them as they are and serve them just as we would serve the most righteous and highly esteemed people we know. This is the very essence of unconditional love.

The fourth step in the process of serving is abiding. Luke records that Jesus stayed at the house of Zacchaeus. He was there long enough for a meal and perhaps even an overnight stay. To serve others best, we must likewise "abide" with them. We must walk in their shoes, see things through their eyes, and be close enough to them and spend enough time with them to be of lasting benefit. Service is not a "hit-and-run" activity.

Jesus made earth His abode for approximately thirty years. God did not send His Son to deliver a quick thirty-second message from a cloud in the sky. Rather, He sent Him to live among men and women and abide with them day in and day out, through all kinds of situations, so that they might truly see Him and know Him fully.

We are called to abide in Christ always—to be in such close relationship with Him and His Word that it is virtually impossible for others to tell where our love ends and His begins (see John 8:31–32; 15:5). At the same time, we are to abide in loving relationship with others—we are to be the "body" of Christ. It is only when we serve others in this way that people can count on us to be there in a time of need. When we abide with others and remain available to them, our witness becomes truly strong and steadfast. We become effective for the gospel when we put down roots and choose to *abide* in relationship with others.

One of the best examples of abiding is found in the early church. Believers banded together when they were ostracized by their families and friends. Many of them lost their jobs, their inheritances, or their social standing. But rather than *from* Christ, they turned *toward* Him and one another. They helped each other in practical ways and formed a community that resulted in adequate provision for all (see Acts 2:44–47). The result was a revival. As people saw how the new Christians loved and cared for one another, they were drawn to Christ.

What was true back then is still true today. When unbelievers see Christians loving and serving one another and reaching out to others in need, they say, "I want to be a part of that group. I want what those people have."

4. "Heal the sick, cleanse the lepers, raise the dead, cast out demons. Freely you have received, freely give" (Matthew 10:8). What, besides your salvation, have you "freely received" from God? How can you share those gifts with others in service to Christ?

5. Think of someone who has chosen to abide with you in steadfast friendship. How does it feel to have that kind of friend? In what ways do you serve one another?

6. "Now all who believed were together, and had all things in common, and sold their possessions and goods, and divided them among all, as anyone had need" (Acts 2:44–45). What does it mean in practical terms to "have all things in common"? How can your church or Bible study group better engage with this concept?

ABANDONMENT

The ultimate step in service is self-abandonment—laying aside all of one's selfish desires and all of one's personal agenda in order to do whatever God asks. When Jesus entered the home of Zacchaeus, He abandoned any concern for His public reputation. He knew the majority of the people in Jericho would accuse Him of aligning with a sinner. Yet He was willing to risk a loss of general public esteem in order to bring salvation to the household of Zacchaeus.

Likewise, in the book of Acts we read how Peter went to the house of Cornelius, abandoning years of prejudice against the Gentiles. Peter was willing to go because it was clear to him that God was calling him to go—even if it meant stepping outside the bounds of his own "comfort zone" (see Acts 10). In the same way, four men carried their paralyzed friend to Jesus on a stretcher and tore a hole in the roof in order to lower him into Jesus' presence when they couldn't get past the crowd in the doorway. They abandoned their own schedules and desires. They let nothing stand in the way of helping their friend get to Jesus (see Mark 2:1–12).

God calls us to abandon our concern for ourselves and focus on serving others. As we do, we actually find true meaning in our lives. This was the message that Jesus had a for a rich young man who came to Him one day and asked, "Good Teacher, what shall I do that I may inherit eternal life?" (Mark 10:17). Jesus reminded him of the commandments, which this man knew and had kept diligently. However, being "good" and religious were not enough.

Jesus called this man to a degree of abandonment in service. He said, "One thing you lack: Go your way, sell whatever you have and give to the poor, and you will have treasure in heaven; and come, take up the cross, and follow Me" (verse 21). Jesus required this man to utterly abandon self—and it is also what He requires of us.

7. "Assuredly, I say to you, there is no one who has left house or brothers or sisters or father or mother or wife or children or lands, for My sake and the gospel's, who shall not receive a hundredfold now in this time—houses and brothers and sisters and mothers and children and lands, with persecutions—and in the age to come, eternal life. But many who are first will be last, and the last first" (Mark 10:29–31). Notice that Jesus adds "with

persecutions" to the list of rewards for service. Why do His people receive persecution when they serve others?

....

....

....

....

....

8. When have you seen the principle of "the first shall be last" at work in real life? When have you *not* seen it work out that way?

....

....

....

....

....

....

WHERE ARE YOU IN YOUR SERVICE?

Once again, the pattern toward full service is *awareness, availability, acceptance, abiding,* and *abandonment.* So, where are you in this pattern of service? To what next step is God calling you? You must become *aware* of the needs of others before you can ever make an effort to meet those needs. You must be *available* if you are to serve. You must *accept* others fully, just as they are, if you are to give them the unconditional love of Christ. It is as you *abide* with others over time that your service becomes steadfast and reliable and your heart is knit to the hearts of others. Finally, as a servant you are called to exercise complete *abandonment*—not merely serving others some of the time, but living in a constant state of outreach to others at all times—on the job, at home, in the community, at church, and wherever God leads.

9. "This is My commandment, that you love one another as I have loved you. Greater love has no one than this, than to lay down one's life for his friends" (John 15:12–13). When have you been called on to serve someone to the point where it felt like you were laying down your life for that person? When has someone done that for you?

10. "Let love be without hypocrisy. Abhor what is evil. Cling to what is good. Be kindly affectionate to one another with brotherly love, in honor giving preference to one another; not lagging in diligence, fervent in spirit, serving the Lord; rejoicing in hope, patient in tribulation, continuing steadfastly in prayer; distributing to the needs of the saints, given to hospitality" (Romans 12:9–13). What does it mean to "let love be without hypocrisy"? When has your love for others been tainted with hypocrisy?

TODAY AND TOMORROW

Today: Jesus demonstrated that service requires awareness, availability, acceptance, abiding, and abandonment.

Tomorrow: I will ask God to show me areas in my life where I need to strengthen one or more of these principles.

CLOSING PRAYER

Lord Jesus, we thank You for not coming into this world as a superstar. Instead, You came as a servant. Thank You for demonstrating for us in the life of Zacchaeus what kind of servant You really are. You did not mind all the criticism that You received—You chose to abandon Yourself of all concern of what people thought from the very beginning. Today, it is our prayer that You will search our hearts and convict us of any area where we are still holding on to pride. Release us from those attitudes and mindsets that keep us from stepping out to serve one another. May we make an honest commitment to follow these five principles of service as You lead us.

NOTES AND
PRAYER REQUESTS

Use this space to write any key points, questions, or prayer requests from this week's study.

QUALITIES OF AN EFFECTIVE SERVANT (PART 1)

Learning: What are the qualities of an effective servant?

Growing: Where will I get these qualities, if I don't have them already?

The early church grew rapidly after the ascension of Jesus . . . and with that growth came new challenges. At one point, a group known as the "Hellenists" (Jewish Christians who had been influenced by Greek culture) began to complain that the widows of the "Hebrews" (Jewish Christians who had maintained Jewish practices) were being shown favoritism at the communal meals held by the church. To resolve the issue, the twelve apostles called a meeting in Jerusalem and commissioned seven men to fulfill the need (see Acts 6:1–6).

The role of these seven men was not the same as that of the apostles, but it was nevertheless considered a vital *ministry* role within the church. These seven men became the first deacons. The word for *deacon* in the Greek language had a different meaning than it does today in most Christian denominations. In many churches, deacons are chosen for their business ability and position in the world. Once they are elected as deacons, they often attempt to fill spiritual roles of leadership. However, these first deacons in the early church were chosen for spiritual qualities—and they were given practical roles of service.

The word for *deacon* in the Greek language is also used to express the concepts "to run" or "to hasten." The first deacons were expected to be quick in their response to the needs of believers. They were given the job of protecting the harmony of the fellowship—of making sure things were done equitably and in order, of making certain all the needs were met, and of ensuring that no cliques developed within the body of Christ. As we look as these men, we see they were chosen on the basis of six qualities. These men were (1) submissive, (2) of good reputation, (3) full of the Holy Spirit, (4) wise, (5) visionaries for the work of God, and (6) humble. These are the same qualities that today make the most effective servants.

1. "Then the twelve summoned the multitude of the disciples and said, 'It is not desirable that we should leave the word of God and serve tables'" (Acts 6:2). What immediate steps did the twelve disciples take to resolve the issue in the church?

2. "Therefore, brethren, seek out from among you seven men of good reputation, full of the Holy Spirit and wisdom, whom we may appoint over this business" (Acts 6:3). Consider the qualities of deacons: submissive, good reputation, filled with the Holy Spirit, wise, committed to God's work, and humble. Which of these qualities do you feel you possess as a servant? Which of these qualities would you like to develop more?

....

....

....

....

....

....

THE QUALITY OF SUBMISSIVENESS

The first deacons were under the authority of apostles. The apostles were the ones who laid hands on the deacons, prayed for them, and imparted to them their authority within the church. In many churches today, this process has been turned upside down—the deacons call the pastors, lay hands on them, and commission them to serve their local church. The order established in the first-century church is more effective and, more important, it is *God's* design.

The apostles were the ones who devoted themselves to prayer and the ministry of the Word. They preached the gospel of Jesus to those who were not yet a part of the fellowship of Christians. They no doubt were also the ones who baptized the new converts when those individuals accepted Christ. The word *apostle* literally means "one sent out," and the apostles filled this role—they were at the cutting edge of the outreach of the church.

The role of the deacons was turned inward toward the believers—they were responsible for running the practical matters in the church. They were men of prayer and students of God's Word, but prayer and preaching were not their primary responsibilities. This does not mean that on occasion a deacon might not speak publicly. Stephen is described in the Bible as a man "full of faith and power" who "did great wonders and signs among the people" (Acts 6:8). He became the first martyr as the result of his speaking boldly about Jesus. However, he did not have preaching and prayer as his job description. He exercised his spiritual gifts in the office of deacon, but his primary role was to oversee the meeting of practical needs in the church.

Effective servants *always* submit their will to those who are in authority over them. We are each in a line of authority. Ultimately, that authority is Christ Jesus. It is only when we learn to submit our wills to His will and to obey those whom God has placed over us that we truly can be effective servants. Rebellious individuals might go through some of the external motions of service for a period of time, but they will not *remain* steadfast servants over time. They cannot be truly effective in helping people grow in their faith or experience an increasing reliance on the Holy Spirit, because they are not totally reliant on the Holy Spirit themselves.

Submission is not a state of groveling or of weakness. Rather, it is recognizing that someone has greater God-given authority in a particular situation. It is yielding one's decision-making power to a higher authority and curbing one's behavior to conform to the rule established by one who occupies a position of authority. In truth, submissiveness and faith are closely linked. If we fail to believe God is going to provide for us, protect us, or work things for good on our behalf, we are unlikely to submit to God or trust Him. However, if we believe God is our heavenly Father and that all He does is ultimately for our eternal good, we are likely to submit to Him, have faith in Him, and trust Him for every detail of our lives.

The first deacons were willing to let the apostles be apostles and take on their own role of service as deacons. They did not try to *lead the church* but *resolved problems within the church* under the authority granted to them by the apostles. As servants today, we are likewise called to submit ourselves to the Holy Spirit and do what He directs us to say and do.

3. "Now when Jesus had entered Capernaum, a centurion came to Him, pleading with Him, saying, 'Lord, my servant is lying at home paralyzed, dreadfully tormented.' And Jesus said to him, 'I will come and heal him.' The centurion answered and said, 'Lord, I am not worthy that You should come under my roof. But only speak a word, and my servant will be healed'" (Matthew 8:5–8). Why did the centurion say he was "not worthy" to have Jesus come to his house? What leadership quality did he demonstrate?

4. "When Jesus heard it, He marveled, and said to those who followed, 'Assuredly, I say to you, I have not found such great faith, not even in Israel!'" (Matthew 8:10). Why do you think Jesus reacted in this manner? How did the centurion reveal his faith?

THE QUALITY OF A GOOD REPUTATION

The deacons were chosen first and foremost because they were "men of good reputation" (Acts 6:3). They had exemplary character and were men of the highest integrity. A good reputation is something that we are to work at achieving and to value highly. Of course, this does not mean that people will totally agree with us at all times. We may also disagree with the decisions made by those of good character and still admire and respect them as people of God.

From the biblical point of view, goodness and godliness are the same. One cannot bear a reputation for goodness without being godly. Goodness is one of the qualities of the Holy Spirit that we are to bear as His fruit in our lives (see Galatians 5:22). While people often judge a person's reputation on the basis of what that person says and does, the fact is that what we believe is inevitably revealed by what we say . . . and what we say inevitably dictates what we do. If we believe God's Word, say we are making God's Word our way of life, and then truly attempt to live out God's Word on a daily basis, we are building a good reputation.

A good reputation has nothing to do with the standards of success established by the world. Being rich, famous, or the leader of an organization does not make a person good or godly. The lowliest wage earner can be a person of excellent reputation. The most unrecognized person within the church might still be a person whom others recognize as godly.

Why is a good reputation so vital for service? Because genuine service is a reflection of God's love and presence. If we are just going through the motions of service with an evil intent or a selfish interest, others will know it. Others will treat us as suspect—and even our service itself as suspect. In our culture today, many people believe that a person's character doesn't matter as long as the outcome is good. From God's standpoint, the character of the person giving the service *is* what makes the outcome of that person's work good.

We cannot separate inner character and outer deeds. In the end, a good reputation is vital to good service.

Our reputation is one of the foremost factors in our witness to the world about the saving grace of God. Our greatest witness for Christ is found in the way that we lead our daily lives. Who we are, from the inside out, is the platform from which we give service. Our service will not redeem us or make our reputation. Our reputation for having a godly character is what will redeem our service and give us a witness for Christ Jesus.

We must also be aware that a good reputation does not necessarily spare a person from persecution (see 2 Timothy 3:12–15). Those who perform good service to others sometimes are criticized for it, misunderstood because of it, or ridiculed as being a "goody two-shoes." However, what can be said for a good reputation is that it survives persecution—even if that persecution leads to death. A good reputation lasts, and it affects others for good. If a person's reputation is a godly one in Christ Jesus, it will last into eternity.

If you want your service to outlive your lifetime and be credited to your eternal reward, you must be a person who strives to achieve and maintain a good reputation. Don't be discouraged if you face persecution or if your reputation is assaulted for the service that you perform. Press on. Your reputation *will* be vindicated eventually, and your service *will* be rewarded by God.

5. How do you feel when someone you don't respect does a good thing for you? What is likely to be your response to the person and to the service rendered to you?

6. "Every good tree bears good fruit, but a bad tree bears bad fruit. A good tree cannot bear bad fruit, nor can a bad tree bear good fruit" (Matthew 7:17–18). How does this image of "bad fruit" relate to acts of service given by someone with mixed motives?

....

....

....

....

....

7. Jesus tells us that a good tree cannot bear bad fruit. What does that suggest about the importance of godliness in your life as you seek to serve others?

....

....

....

....

....

....

THE QUALITY OF BEING FULL OF THE HOLY SPIRIT

The apostles requested the members of the Jerusalem church choose as deacons men who were "full of the Holy Spirit" (Acts 6:3). The Holy Spirit is the One who guides us as believers in Christ into good words, good works, and a good walk before our heavenly Father. He is the One who enables us to perform good works that have a lasting benefit to the kingdom of God. It is impossible to do anything on earth that is of eternal value unless the Holy Spirit enables us to do that work.

God alone knows which of our works has the potential to be the most effective and productive in His kingdom. He alone guarantees that our work will succeed in spite of persecution and our own failures. God alone can cause a work of service to become a point of witness to a lost soul and can use our service to redeem lives for all eternity. God alone can assure us of an eternal reward for our service. Without God, nothing that we do can be remotely as important, beneficial, or lasting as what we can do *with* God.

We already mentioned that Stephen was a man "full of faith and the Holy Spirit" and "full of faith and power" (Acts 6:5, 8). What an amazing and wonderful reputation to have! To be *full* of God's Spirit means that Stephen's life was overflowing and continuously demonstrating the character of God. He was a man who embodied all of the fruit of the Spirit described by Paul: "love, joy, peace, longsuffering, kindness, goodness, faithfulness, gentleness, self-control" (Galatians 5:22–23). Paul also wrote that there is nothing in the law—either God's law or man's law—that prohibits a person from having these traits. They are qualities of character that are desirable in *all* people, in *all* periods of history, and in young and old alike.

Servant who are full of the Holy Spirit are like Jesus. Servants filled with the Holy Spirit are those who say what Jesus would say in any situation, do what Jesus would do in any circumstance, and live as Jesus would live in any environment. Servants who are full of the Holy Spirit are obviously those who are completely submissive to the Holy Spirit for direction, guidance, and power. They do nothing that the Holy Spirit does not prompt and enable. They are totally reliant on God for every move that they make.

Christians often say to one another, "If only Jesus were here, He would solve this problem." But the truth is that if we are truly full of the same Holy Spirit that filled Jesus, it is as if Jesus is in our midst. And our collective service or ministry to others will be just as effective and meaningful as if that person were touched by the very hands of Christ Jesus, heard the very words of Christ Jesus, or received the very gifts that Christ Jesus would give.

When we attempt to serve others without relying on the Holy Spirit, we burn out, become discouraged at failures and trials, and often become lax in our service and weak in our desire to serve. None of us can remain faithful, devoted, and consistent in our service without the Holy Spirit's help. To be truly effective in our service to others, we *must* ask the Holy Spirit to work in us and through us—today, tomorrow, and every day in our future.

8. When have you attempted to do a "good work" without relying on the Holy Spirit? What were the long-range results—for you as well as for those you served?

....

....

....

....

....

....

....

9. When have you been completely reliant on the Holy Spirit in your service? What were the long-range results—for you and for those you served?

....

....

....

....

....

....

....

....

10. "But the Helper, the Holy Spirit, whom the Father will send in My name, He will teach you all things, and bring to your remembrance all things that I said to you" (John 14:26). How has the Holy Spirit helped you to think, act, and be like Christ?

....

....

....

....

....

TODAY AND TOMORROW

Today: An effective servant is first and foremost filled with the presence of the Holy Spirit.

Tomorrow: I will prayerfully strive to strengthen the fruit of the Spirit in my own life.

CLOSING PRAYER

Heavenly Father, Your Word has provided a guide for us to follow in what it means to possess the qualities of an effective servant. We want to follow in the footsteps of those first deacons in the early church who were submissive to You, of good reputation, and filled with the power of the Holy Spirit. Thank You for loving us enough to take us with our faults, our frailties, and our mistakes when we don't live up to these standards. So often we feel so inadequate to carry out what You have asked of us. But as we look to the example of Stephen and others, help us to remember that they were humans just like us. Let us always be willing to follow where You lead.

NOTES AND PRAYER REQUESTS

Use this space to write any key points, questions, or prayer requests from this week's study.

QUALITIES OF AN EFFECTIVE SERVANT (PART 2)

IN THIS LESSON

Learning: How do wisdom, vision, and humility affect my service?

Growing: Where do those qualities come from?

In the last lesson, we covered three traits that we are to embody in our service: *submissiveness*, a *good reputation*, and a *life filled with the Holy Spirit*. In this lesson, we will cover the remaining traits that are vital for an effective servant of God to possess: *wisdom, vision,* and *humility*. These character qualities are vital for effective service within the church, but they are effective in serving others outside the church in order to bring them to Christ.

A godly person who simultaneously has a submissive human spirit and is filled with the power of the Holy Spirit is an extremely effective witness for Christ. Such a person has a tremendous role in the growth and development of God's kingdom—regardless of their particular position in life. Show me a godly custodian who is submissive and filled with God's Holy Spirit, and I will show you a person who makes a lasting difference for good. Show me a pastor who has an "I-can-do-it-on-my-own" attitude and who is not reliant on the Holy Spirit, and I will show you a person who is probably in error in various areas. The reputation, attitude, and lack of the fruit of the Holy Spirit in this pastor's life will eventually harm the church.

No matter what job you hold, you are called to be a servant who embodies the character traits that were required of the first deacons. If you are to serve others and do so effectively, then you must bear the same spiritual integrity that they manifested.

1. What comes to mind when you consider the qualities of wisdom, vision, and humility?

2. In what ways are you feeling challenged to serve others as the first-century deacons did?

THE QUALITY OF WISDOM

The first deacons were to not only be filled with the Holy Spirit but also with wisdom (see Acts 6:3). *Wisdom* involves both knowing what God desires to do and how God desires the job to be done—and then having the courage to actually *do* what is required. Stated another way, what we do and the degree to which our actions are successful will be a measure of our wisdom.

We cannot be wise and say nothing or do nothing. After all, how will anybody know we are wise? How will *we* know we are wise? Wisdom is not simply having head knowledge. It is having *application* knowledge—knowing how, when, and where to apply our knowledge of God's purposes, plans, and commandments. Wisdom is knowledge that is lived out, acted on, and made useful to real-life decisions.

Wisdom comes from God. It flows from the Holy Spirit to us as we rely on Him to provide it. God doesn't pour out His wisdom on people who do not want it or request it. At the same time, He is more than willing to pour out His wisdom in generous portions on those who desire it and ask for it. So, if you want more wisdom, ask God to give it to you!

Wisdom is vital for service—especially for service in the church—because without it we cannot discern *God's* answers to our problems. We can render service based solely on our own desires and employing our own human levels of intelligence and ability—but such service will be limited and often in error. Just imagine what would have happened if the early church simply chose the *smartest* men they knew rather than the *wisest* men they knew. It would have been a catastrophe, because they would have had seven "intelligent" opinions about how to serve and what to do, but no consensus in the Spirit and no true unity in purpose, plan, or result.

Wisdom is something that you need on a daily basis. So ask the Holy Spirit every morning to give you the wisdom that you will need to deal with the circumstances and situations you will face in the coming day. As you face particular decisions, ask the Holy Spirit to guide you. As you encounter people throughout your day, ask the Holy Spirit to direct your conversation. You can never ask too much or too often for God's wisdom!

Ask for such wisdom in faith, and then make the decision or take the action that you believe God has called you to do. Don't second-guess God or yourself at that point. God will reveal to you if you have erred. The only way to grow in your ability to apply God's Word effectively is to obey what God's Word says. Finally, keep in mind always that the Holy Spirit will never direct you to do something that is contrary to the Bible.

3. "If any of you lacks wisdom, let him ask of God, who gives to all liberally and without reproach, and it will be given to him. But let him ask in faith, with no doubting, for he who doubts is like a wave of the sea driven and tossed by the wind" (James 1:5-6). How does James describe a person who doubts when making a request to God? How does James say that we are to ask God for wisdom?

....

....

....

....

4. "The fear of the LORD is the beginning of wisdom, and the knowledge of the Holy One is understanding" (Proverbs 9:10). How would you describe the "fear of the LORD"? What does it look like when the fear of the Lord is a part of your life?

....

....

....

....

THE QUALITY OF VISION

The deacons chosen by the early church were men who also had a vision for what God desired to be done in their midst. They were not attempting to fulfill their own desires or goals but the desires of God's heart for His people. True service always has an evangelistic aspect that is borne of a vision for what God desires to do on the earth. We each are responsible for winning as many people as possible to Christ Jesus in our generation. When we have this at the core of our desire to serve, everything we do takes on greater meaning.

People with a vision for the greater plans and purposes of God understand the reason God has called them to serve. We are not to feed people simply to feed people. We are to feed the hungry so that, with full stomachs, they might fully receive the gospel of Christ. We are not to provide clothing, shelter, or medical help to people merely so they can be warm and live longer. We are to engage in these forms of service so they might not have any barriers that keep them from hearing God's call of grace and forgiveness to them.

True Christian service involves removing the obstacles that keep people from having "ears to hear" and "eyes to see." After all, if the deacons in the early church had not performed practical and daily acts of service, it is likely that large numbers of needy Christians would have fallen away from their newfound faith. The Christian life would simply have been too difficult for them to maintain—their needs would have loomed so large that they would not have been able to hear the full message of the gospel.

A vision grows in us when we ask *why* God has called us to serve. We see the bigger picture: God desires to meet the needs of all people and show His love in tangible ways. He blesses His people materially, practically, and physically as much as He blesses them spiritually. Often we place such great importance on God's spiritual blessings that we neglect to give importance to God's material blessings to those who are lacking the basics necessary for life.

Jesus said that He came not only to give us eternal life but also an abundant life in the here and now (see John 10:10). As His servants, we are to provide service that leads both to an abundant life on this earth and to a spiritual life that is everlasting. One form of service is not to be replaced by the other. We are to have a vision for the greater service—leading a person to Christ—as we engage diligently in performing the practical service of meeting daily needs.

5. "If I do not do the works of My Father, do not believe Me; but if I do, though you do not believe Me, believe the works, that you may know and believe that the Father is in Me, and I in Him" (John 10:37-38). What "works of the Father" did Jesus perform during His earthly ministry?

....

....

....

....

....

....

6. How did Jesus' works of service to others reveal to the people around Him that He was doing God's work?

....

....

....

....

....

....

THE QUALITY OF HUMILITY

Perhaps the supreme character trait of the first-century deacons was humility. These men were filled with faith and power, they had a vision for God's work, and they had outstanding reputations—yet they were asked to *serve tables*. They were asked to become, in effect, waiters. They were responsible for making certain that everyone at the church's communal meals received enough food and that their needs were met without prejudice or favoritism.

Many of the most important roles in the church today are roles similar to that of serving tables. Show me ushers, greeters, parking attendants, and janitors who do their work with the same spirit as that of the first deacons, and I will show you a church that is headed for great effectiveness in the winning of souls and the building up of the body of Christ.

Humility is at the foundation of submissiveness. It is the complement to wisdom—it is what keeps the wise from becoming arrogant. Humility is a sign of being filled with the Holy Spirit and a hallmark of those who have good reputations. Humility says, "Not my will, but Your will." It is the trait that opens our eyes to the broader vision that God has for our lives.

Humility will cause us to see every task as a "job" to be done for God, rather than as a "position" to be filled to win the approval of others. In serving tables, the deacons had as their goal to see that everyone was being taken care of—which is one of the best definitions of service that I have ever heard. When we serve an individual, we are actually serving the greater body of Christ. Any form of service that we desire to render to the church as a whole must first be done for an individual.

It is not enough that people be fed once. They must be fed consistently so that hunger is no longer a part of their daily concern. It is not enough that people be greeted warmly on one Sunday a year. They must feel welcome within the church body every time they set foot inside the church or encounter a member of the church. It is not enough that people be told the gospel once. They must be presented with the gospel at all times—in every word, by every deed, and through every action that is taken on their behalf.

Humility calls us to see the *person* who needs our help, not the *crowd* who might shower adoration upon us. Pride and service are incompatible. Compare the two:

Pride	Service
Self-seeking	Seeks out the best for others
Insists on having my own way	Makes a way for others
Demands recognition	Works for results
Fills us self-importance	Empties us of self

If we are willing to bow our knees before God, we must also be willing to get down on our knees to help others. Humility before God must extend to our having a humble spirit toward others.

7. "Likewise you younger people, submit yourselves to your elders. Yes, all of you be submissive to one another, and be clothed with humility, for 'God resists the proud, but gives grace to the humble'" (1 Peter 5:5). What does it mean to be "clothed with humility"? How is this different from being clothed with pride?

8. "Therefore humble yourselves under the mighty hand of God, that He may exalt you in due time." (1 Peter 5:6). How does a person humble himself or herself "under the mighty hand of God"? What is the result when the person chooses this course?

....

....

....

....

....

....

....

THE RESULT OF GENUINE SERVICE

Luke tells us the result of the church's choosing deacons who bore these six qualities of an effective servant: "The word of God spread, and the number of the disciples multiplied greatly in Jerusalem, and a great many of the priests were obedient to the faith" (Acts 6:7). A church that is filled with people who are active in their service one to another is a church that is like a great magnet to lost souls. The reputation of that church spreads quickly. Christ is lifted up on the shoulders of men and women who are kneeling to perform good service to others. He draws the lost to Himself through the extended arms of believers.

Note that Luke states "a great many of the *priests* became obedient to the faith." The service of the deacons became an example to the believers. They, in turn, began to serve one another with generous, humble, submissive spirits that were open to the Holy Spirit's wisdom and power. As the believers began to serve, the outside world took notice. The entire atmosphere of Jerusalem changed. Many of those who were engaged in the priestly functions of the temple actually began to claim Jesus as the Messiah.

If you want to bring joy to the heart of your pastor, serve others in your church as if you were serving Jesus Himself. Pour out your love to your fellow believers. Your example will draw unbelievers to your church, and your pastor will be encouraged as never before. Nothing warms the heart of a pastor more than to see those in his congregation loving one another. Likewise, if you want to see church growth, also begin with service. It flows automatically from hearts that bear the qualities of submissiveness, godly character, wisdom, a vision for God's work, humility, and a desire to be filled to overflowing with God's Spirit.

9. "But if you have bitter envy and self-seeking in your hearts, do not boast and lie against the truth. This wisdom does not descend from above, but is earthly, sensual, demonic. For where envy and self-seeking exist, confusion and every evil thing are there" (James 3:14–16). What are some examples of worldly wisdom that proves it is earthly, sensual, and demonic? What are the results of following such wisdom?

10. "But the wisdom that is from above is first pure, then peaceable, gentle, willing to yield, full of mercy and good fruits, without partiality and without hypocrisy" (James 3:17). What are some examples of godly wisdom that proves it is pure, peaceable, gentle,

submissive, full of mercy and good fruits, and without partiality or hypocrisy? What are the results of following such wisdom?

....

....

....

....

....

....

TODAY AND TOMORROW

Today: The first-century deacons were men of wisdom, humility, and vision.

Tomorrow: I will seek the Holy Spirit's help this week in developing these vital qualities.

CLOSING PRAYER

Lord, call us today to examine our hearts and ask the question as to whether we truly have a servant spirit. We want to be submissive to You, have a good reputation, and be filled with the Spirit. But we also desire to possess the traits of wisdom, vision, and humility. We thank and praise You for giving us so many opportunities to serve. May we count our blessings again and again . . . and again . . . for the privilege of serving wherever You have called us to serve. May we love others with all our hearts and to the best of the abilities that You have given to us.

NOTES AND
PRAYER REQUESTS

· ·

Use this space to write any key points, questions, or prayer requests from this week's study.

Equipped for Service

Learning: What if I don't have any gifts? What if I am the one who needs comforting?

Growing: How can I use my own experiences to serve others?

People offer many excuses for not engaging in active service to others. Some say they don't have time, while others say they have other priorities. However, there are two basic reasons at the *root* of why people do not serve. *The first is pride.* Often, people do not want to humble themselves to serve. This selfishness is a form of pride— they don't want to be inconvenienced or detoured from what they want to do and when they want to do it. *A second reason is a fear of failure.* Many people feel they do not have anything to give to others or that others will not be open to receiving what they can offer. Both of these reasons lead to unfortunate results.

1. "Love suffers long and is kind; love does not envy; love does not parade itself, is not puffed up" (1 Corinthians 13:4). What does Paul mean when he says that love is not "puffed up"? How does selfishness get in the way of serving others?

2. "God has not given us a spirit of fear, but of power and of love and of a sound mind" (2 Timothy 1:7). How does fear of failure get in the way of serving others?

CONSEQUENCES OF REFUSING TO SERVE

First, those who steadfastly refuse to engage in service do not understand the heart of God. If we truly understand that God is a loving and generous Father—One who gave His only Son so that we might be reconciled to Him and live with Him forever—then we will have a built-in desire to give. After all, how can we know the extent of God's love and *not* want to share it with others? God not only requires us to give service, but He also *desires* for us to give service. If we know that God is love, then we know that we must love others, since God's Spirit resides within us. This means serving others and giving to them in order to meet their needs.

Second, those who steadfastly refuse to engage in service do not understand why they are alive. So many people today ask, "Why am I here?" However, as believers in Christ, we should never have to ask that question. As followers of Jesus, we are here on this earth to worship God and reflect glory to Him by the way we serve. God's command is to love Him and love others just as we love our own life. It is our purpose, role, and meaning in life.

Third, those who steadfastly refuse to engage in service do not understand God's purpose for this world. God's will for the world is that all people might come to know Him and receive forgiveness through Christ. Jesus came to seek and to save *all* who are lost. God's purpose for us as a part of the larger body of Christ is that we be a part of an ongoing and consistent effort to win lost souls to Christ and to build up the faith of our fellow Christians. God's desire is that His kingdom be established on earth, just as it is in heaven. Jesus taught us to pray, "Our Father in heaven, hallowed be Your name. Your kingdom come. Your will be done on earth as it is in heaven" (Matthew 6:9–10).

If we truly understand the heart of God, why we are on this earth, and what God's purposes are for humankind, how can we dare to say to God, "I would rather do my own thing than serve You by serving others"? How can we dare to exert our own will over God's will?

I have more compassion for those who do not believe they have any talents to give than for those who know they are talented yet refuse to use those talents for God's glory. My word to those who believe they don't have anything to offer in the way of service is that *you do*. God does not call anyone to do anything in His kingdom unless He also equips that person—spiritually, materially, physically, financially, and in all other ways.

Whatever type of service God may be opening up to you, know that He has prepared you and equipped you to succeed in doing it. He will also continue to assist you and increase your talents as you engage in the work set before you.

3. "Beloved, let us love one another, for love is of God" (1 John 4:7). How does serving help you to understand the heart of God? How does it help you know your purpose on earth?

....

....

....

....

....

....

....

....

4. "As each one has received a gift, minister it to one another, as good stewards of the manifold grace of God" (1 Peter 4:10). How can serving help you understand God's purposes? How can serving others ultimately bring glory to God?

....

....

....

....

....

....

....

CREATED FOR SERVICE

Service is a part of God's reason for creating us. As the apostle Paul writes, "We are His workmanship, created in Christ Jesus for good works, which God prepared beforehand that we should walk in them" (Ephesians 2:10). Even before we were born, God had in mind who we would be and what He would have us do in this specific time right now.

We haven't arrived where we are in our lives by accident or whim. God's plan and purpose for us are unfolding. God would not have us engage in service for Him without preparing us for the challenge. Our service is thus an outgrowth of the talents and abilities that God has placed in our lives. We each have been given certain "service-ready equipment" from birth: a unique personality, mental and emotional capacities, talents, and strengths.

God has been at work in our lives from our first moments, molding and preparing us to fulfill His plan and purposes. Throughout our lives, God has allowed us to have certain experiences, engage in certain relationships, and be a part of certain groups of people in certain environments and cultures—all of which become a part of the mix of who we are and what we bring to any form of ministry or service. We can be assured that He will continue to work in us until the day we die. God works in us and through us as we serve, and He uses our service to prepare us for even greater service in the days ahead.

You may feel that you are at the kindergarten level of service—that you have limited resources and abilities with which to serve. God's plan is that you use what you have been given to the fullest and, as you use those abilities, He will *increase* them so that you are able to serve Him with greater abilities. God's purpose for you in service is never to decrease you but to increase you and to cause you to prosper in all areas of your life—mentally, physically, emotionally, materially, and, above all, spiritually.

5. "He who has begun a good work in you will complete it until the day of Jesus Christ" (Philippians 1:6). Notice God will complete His work in us *until* the day of Jesus Christ," rather than "*by* the day of Jesus Christ." What does this suggest about God's involvement in our lives? What does this suggest about our part in God's work?

....

....

....

....

....

....

....

....

....

....

....

6. What talents and skills has God given you? How can those skills be used to serve others?

....

....

....

....

....

....

....

....

....

....

....

....

EQUIPPED WITH SPIRITUAL GIFTS

Not only have we been equipped with certain gifts and abilities, but the Holy Spirit also dwells within us. He brings to us His unlimited gifts and abilities! This is why Paul could claim, "I can do all things through Christ who strengthens me" (Philippians 4:13). What we lack, the Holy Spirit supplies. When we are weak, He is strong. When we fail in our service to others, He continues to work all things together for good—to us and to those whom we serve (see Romans 8:28). We are guaranteed to be successful in our service as long as we rely on the Holy Spirit to work in us, through us, and on our behalf—both individually and as members of the greater body of Christ.

As Paul states, there are several gifts the Holy Spirit freely gives to those who believe in Christ: "Having then gifts differing according to the grace that is given to us, let us use them: if prophecy, let us prophesy in proportion to our faith; or ministry, let us use it in our ministering; he who teaches, in teaching; he who exhorts, in exhortation; he who gives, with liberality; he who leads, with diligence; he who shows mercy, with cheerfulness" (Romans 12:6–8).

Note that Paul's emphasis is on the *use* of spiritual gifts. We do not receive these gifts from the Holy Spirit for our exclusive benefit but so that others might be blessed and, in the process, we might grow in our faith and spiritual power. Furthermore, it is the *Holy Spirit* who determines which gift He will choose to put into operation at any given time in our lives and service to others. The gifts of the Spirit are just that—the Spirit's gifts. They reside in Him and are given to us for the greater use of the entire body of Christ. As Paul states, "The manifestation of the Spirit is given to each one for the profit of all" (1 Corinthians 12:7).

God gives you supernatural gifts so that you might serve others. So, if you feel a need in your service to another person, ask God to endow you with whatever gift you need in order to get *His* job done for *His* glory. He will do so! He is the One who gives spiritual gifts so that

His people might be edified and His kingdom expanded and His love and grace revealed to the lost.

7. "Now may He who supplies seed to the sower, and bread for food, supply and multiply the seed you have sown and increase the fruits of your righteousness, while you are enriched in everything for all liberality, which causes thanksgiving through us to God" (2 Corinthians 9:10–11). According to these verses, who is responsible for creating the "seed" of service to others? Who is responsible for sowing that seed?

....

....

....

....

....

8. What benefit does the sower receive for sowing the seed? What is the *purpose* of that benefit to the sower?

....

....

....

....

....

....

THE PURPOSE OF GIFTS

As Paul wrote to the believers in Corinth, "The God and Father of our Lord Jesus Christ . . . comforts us in all our tribulation, that we may be able to comfort those who are in any trouble, with the comfort with which we ourselves are comforted by God" (2 Corinthians 1:3–4). The gifts of the Holy Spirit are intended for us to use in comforting those who are in trouble. As we have been comforted by Christ, so we are to comfort others.

All of our experiences in life—especially those who have brought us pain, sorrow, and suffering—equip us in unique ways to have empathy with others and to show compassion to them. Everything in your life—even your failures and suffering—has prepared you to show the love of God to others. God's grace to you in your times of suffering prepares you to become an effective minister of God to those who are currently suffering.

Too often, people in the church expect the pastor to do all of the ministering to those who have emotional or spiritual needs. But this is far from what the Bible sets as the standard for service. As Paul wrote to the believers in Ephesus, "To each one of us grace was given according to the measure of Christ's gift . . . He Himself gave some to be apostles, some prophets, some evangelists, and some pastors and teachers, for the equipping of the saints for the work of ministry, for the edifying of the body of Christ" (Ephesians 4:7, 11–12).

The leaders in any church setting have been placed there for one main reason: *to equip the saints for the work of ministry*. If you are a layperson, you are a saint who is being equipped for ministry. Your purpose is not to listen to hundreds of sermons and attend dozens of seminars and then die and go to heaven. Your purpose is to hear the Word of God as it is preached and then immediately and consistently to apply that preaching and teaching in practical forms of service to the people around you. The "work" of ministry belongs to all of God's people. In ministering to others, you become an agent of God's comfort and care.

It is out of thanksgiving for what God has done that you serve others. If you have been forgiven by God and are the recipient of God's love, then you *are* equipped for service. He will provide what you lack in ability.

9. "For it is God who works in you both to will and to do for His good pleasure" (Philippians 2:13). According to this verse, what effect does God's will have on your will and desires when you are in fellowship with Him?

10. How might this require you to change your own plans at times?

TODAY AND TOMORROW

Today: God sends everything into my life—even sorrow—for the purpose of serving others.

Tomorrow: I will ask God to show me this week how I can use my own life experiences to serve others.

CLOSING PRAYER

Heavenly Father, we marvel when we consider that we are Your workmanship and have been created for good works that You prepared beforehand for us to do. It is amazing that even before we took our first breath on this earth, You already had in mind who we would be and what tasks You would set before us. Thank You for such tangible demonstrations of Your love and power. When we stand before You when our time in this world is finished, we want You to see a lifetime of works, characterized by You as gold and silver and precious stone.

NOTES AND
PRAYER REQUESTS

Use this space to write any key points, questions, or prayer requests from this week's study.

FIVE PRINCIPLES OF SUCCESSFUL SERVICE

IN THIS LESSON

Learning: How do I determine the success and results of my own service?

Growing: Who am I supposed to be serving?

Service is a theme that runs throughout God's Word. The Bible is filled with countless examples of God's service to His people, ways in which God's people served God and others, and commandments that are related to service. In this lesson, we are going to take a look at five principles from God's Word that are related to service. These principles are interrelated and should be taken as a whole. God has made it clear in His Word that He *requires* service from us. Service is not an option or a suggestion. It is a commandment.

Service is also our way to increased blessing and fulfillment in life. God does not command us to serve so that we might be diminished or made to suffer. Rather, God commands us to serve so that He might reward us, bring us blessing, teach us, and develop a closer relationship with us. God always rewards our service with more of His presence and power and, ultimately, with eternal rewards that are beyond our ability to imagine.

Jesus said, "A servant is not greater than his master; nor is he who is sent greater than he who sent him. If you know these things, blessed are you if you do them" (John 13:16–17). We *must* serve. But this is a command that we should delight in obeying because service always reaps benefit—to us personally as well as to those whom we serve.

PRINCIPLE 1: VOLUNTEERISM

True servants don't wait to be asked. They discern a need and act decisively to meet it. They have sensitive hearts and willing spirits. They are motivated by love and are prompted to action by the presence of a need. True servants are *not* motivated by convenience or leisure time. Those who say, "someday I will get involved," or, "someday I will serve God," are offering lame excuses. They will *never* end up serving if they are waiting for a convenient time to do so.

There are two questions we can ask ourselves to reveal our own self pride: (1) "What is it that I won't do for God?" and (2) "What is it that I wouldn't do for another person?" Remember that Jesus died naked, bloody, and battered on a cross that was next to a public highway. He was made a laughingstock—a crown of thorns pressed into His brow and a sign above His head mocking Him as "King of the Jews." Jesus died for *our* sake so that we might have a Savior.

Furthermore, Jesus went to the cross voluntarily. As He said shortly before His crucifixion, "I am the good shepherd; and I know My sheep, and am known by My own. As the Father knows Me, even so I know the Father; and I lay down My life for the sheep. . . . I lay down My life that I may take it again. No one takes it from Me, but I lay it down of Myself. I have power to lay it down, and I have power to take it again. This command I have received from My Father" (John 10:14–15, 17–18).

Jesus was obedient to His heavenly Father, and the cross was His supreme act of volunteerism. He *gave* His life voluntarily for our salvation without regard to pain, suffering, mockery, or the disbelief of many who witnessed His death.

Is there any type of service that is beneath you? Is there anything you won't do for God? The Lord said about King David: "I have found David the son of Jesse, a man after My own heart, who will do all My will" (Acts 13:22). Will God say that about you?

1. "But without your consent I wanted to do nothing, that your good deed might not be by compulsion, as it were, but voluntary" (Philemon 1:14). How is a person's service different if it is done voluntarily rather than by compulsion?

2. Why would Paul want to ensure that Philemon was serving voluntarily? Why not just force him into it and get the job done?

PRINCIPLE 2: WITHOUT COMPARISON

True servants do not compare their type of service with that of anyone else. Service is not hierarchical. There is no "top floor, corner office" when it comes to successful service. God looks on the heart and its motivation in rewarding service, not on results or achievements.

As we discussed in the last lesson, every person is capable and qualified for some type of service. Many people say, "I would do more for God if I only had . . ." and then fill in the blank with different excuses, such as, "a different job and income," or, "different circumstances and time availability," or, "a different family background and status."

However, everything you have is a gift from God, and what you have been given is adequate for the tasks to which God calls you. So, rather than focus on what you lack, take a look at what you *have*. Not only do you have adequate talents and gifts with which to serve, but God has also given you a place and a people to serve. God has given you your family, your place of employment, your friends, your church, and your neighborhood as opportunities to serve. There are needs all around you. Target *one* of them and get started.

Once you begin to serve, don't criticize those who fail to serve. Jesus did not wash the feet of His disciples and then say, "Now you must wash My feet." Service must be without criticism and without comparison. So encourage your fellow servants and build them up, knowing the one who gives encouragement will also receive encouragement. Offer suggestions when you think they may be beneficial to the group as a whole, but don't criticize what people have done in the past or what they are attempting to do now. You never know the full story. Only God knows the full extent of each person's effort and the motivation behind it.

3. "For we dare not class ourselves or compare ourselves with those who commend themselves. But they, measuring themselves by themselves, and comparing themselves among themselves, are not

wise" (2 Corinthians 10:12). What does Paul say that believers in Christ are not to do? What is the danger of such comparison?

....

....

....

....

4. Why are you "not wise" if you compare yourself with those who are around you?

....

....

....

....

PRINCIPLE 3: NO EXCLUSIONS

If people volunteer to join you in your service to others, allow them the privilege of doing so. No one is ever too young or too old to serve. In fact, there is no retirement program for Christian service. Following the Lord's example, we are to serve the Lord and to serve others every day of our lives.

Jesus called His disciples "little children" during the Last Supper and said to them, "A new commandment I give to you, that you love one another; as I have loved you, that you also love one another. By this all will know that you are My disciples, if you have love for one another" (John 13:34–35). Love knows no age limitations. Even a young child is capable of expressing love and care to others.

Just as you should not exclude anyone from an opportunity to serve, you must also not exclude anyone from receiving service. Consider all the people whom the Lord Jesus touched with His hands. These included a leper, a child, and a blind man. Jesus used His hands to wash the feet of His disciples. Eventually, He spread His hands out on a cross and died for the sins of all humankind. He certainly expects you to extend your hands to those in need regardless of their race, color, culture, or type of need.

5. When have you been excluded from receiving or giving service? How did you feel?

....

....

....

....

6. "Therefore, from now on, we regard no one according to the flesh" (2 Corinthians 5:16). What does it mean to "regard someone according to the flesh"? When have you treated someone differently because of some "fleshly element"?

....

....

....

....

Principle 4: Commitment

Regardless of whether or not you have been committed to service in the past, you can make a new start today. Ask God to forgive you for any wasted opportunities to serve. Make a commitment to yourself to discover your talents and abilities that might be used in service. Then make a commitment to get involved in the lives of others to help and provide as you are able. A real commitment is one that is acted on . . . not merely one that is talked about.

Commitment is required if you are to endure in your service through difficult times. As Paul wrote, "If anyone builds on this foundation with gold, silver, precious stones, wood, hay, straw, each one's work will become clear; for the Day will declare it, because it will be revealed by fire; and the fire will test each one's work, of what sort it is. If anyone's work which he has built on it endures, he will receive a reward" (1 Corinthians 3:12–14).

Make certain that what you do with your time, energy, and talent is for the gospel and that your work will be counted as gold, silver, and precious stones. It is what you do for your own self-serving interests and self-gratification that will be revealed as wood, hay, and straw.

7. "Commit your way to the LORD, trust also in Him, and He shall bring it to pass" (Psalm 37:5). What does it mean to commit your way to the Lord? What does this involve?

8. "Whatever you do, do it heartily, as to the Lord and not to men" (Colossians 3:23). How can viewing everything you do as an act of service to the Lord change your outlook on helping others? How can this help you stay committed to service?

PRINCIPLE 5: THE OUTCOME BELONGS TO GOD

You are not responsible for the outcomes of your service. Your responsibility is to serve God and others to the best of your ability, with the full force of your love, energy, and talents. What happens as the result of your service is God's responsibility.

The apostle Paul suffered greatly in giving service to the early church. His ministry was filled with conflict, struggles, and trials.

If you were to evaluate Paul's ministry on the basis of the number of times he was beaten, imprisoned, ridiculed, and scorned, you would consider his ministry to be a total failure. However, the value of Paul's ministry was not measured by what he went through but by what God accomplished through his consistent and persistent teaching of the gospel of Jesus Christ.

It is God who saves souls—you merely do the witnessing. It is God who heals and restores—you merely do the "medicating," the praying, and the exhorting. It is God who delivers—you merely proclaim the power, the blood, and the promises made available to you through the name of Jesus. When you serve, God works. He uses everything that you do for His good purposes and eternal plan.

God calls you to be faithful. Your "success" is up to Him. Ministry is not something that you do *for* God but something God does *through you*. He is the One who calls you to service, enables you to serve, and produces His desired result. So this week, ask the Lord to show you ways to serve others, and then pray He will take care of the results. The rest is up to Him.

9. "[Jesus said,] 'The Father who dwells in Me does the works'" (John 14:10). Jesus is both God and man, yet He Himself depended on the Father to produce results from His service. What does this teach you about your own service?

....

....

....

....

....

10. "Whoever is of a willing heart, let him bring it as an offering to the Lord.... They came, both men and women, as many as had a willing heart" (Exodus 35:5, 22). Why does God want you to have

a willing heart before you serve Him? What should you do if you find that you do *not* have a willing heart to serve?

....

....

....

....

....

TODAY AND TOMORROW

Today: Jesus teaches that I should have a willing heart
to serve anyone that God sends my way.

Tomorrow: I will strive this week to serve willingly,
leaving the results in God's hands.

CLOSING PRAYER

Lord Jesus, keep us ever mindful that it was You who got down on Your knees and washed dusty feet. Let us not forget that You performed the ultimate act of service on our behalf when You willingly accepted the penalty for our sins on the cross. Deliver us from ever thinking that we are too important to do those necesary tasks that may appear, at first, to be tedious, insignificant, or unrewarding. Help us to embody these five principles of servanthood—volunteering, serving without comparison, excluding no one, remaining committed, and trusting that the outcome and results of our actions belong exclusively to You. Let us be willing servants for You.

NOTES AND PRAYER REQUESTS

· ·

Use this space to write any key points, questions, or prayer requests from this week's study.

AVOIDING BURNOUT IN GOD'S SERVICE

IN THIS LESSON

Learning: Why do God's servants often grow weary and walk away from doing His work?

Growing: How can I serve God through His strength rather than my own?

Every year, an increasing number of men and women who have been in the ministry for a long time decide to quit. These are people who have dedicated their lives to serving God, yet they walk away. There are many reasons as to why this happens, but when you talk to these people—and I have personally talked to many of them over the years—they often say the same kinds of things. They talk about growing tired, weary, and worn out. They talk about carrying too much pressure. They say, "I just can't handle it anymore."

We have a word for this phenomenon: *burnout*. You have probably heard this term, and you have probably heard of pastors leaving their churches after becoming burned out. But burnout doesn't just happen to pastors . . . not by a long shot. There are laypeople all over the world who cut back on their service to God because they feel they can no longer handle what they believe God wants them to do. They say, "I just need a break," or, "It's time for me to focus on other areas of my life." Believe me when I say that burnout is a rampant issue that can affect any and all Christians who are seeking to serve God.

For this reason, I believe this topic is important to our exploration of how to develop a servant's heart. Specifically, I want to explore how we can avoid growing weary and burning out even in the most intense seasons of our service in God's kingdom.

1. What would you identify as contributing factors to burnout or people feeling overstressed in service to God?

2. When have you gone through a particularly intense season when you felt drained or weary?

DON'T GO IN YOUR OWN STRENGTH

I learned a great lesson about burnout some time ago. I did not learn this in seminary, and I certainly didn't pick it up from a book. Rather, I learned it at an airport. I was there to pick up a seventy-three-year-old lady named Bertha Smith. She had been scheduled to speak at my church, which at that time was the First Baptist Church in Miami, Florida.

Bertha had spent more than forty years as a missionary in China. I had heard some incredible stories about her ministry—not only about the impact she had made in China but also about the struggles she had endured. She had ministered her way through bombings, attacks, political pressure, financial struggles. You name it . . . she had been through it.

So, when she got off the plane, I said, "Bertha, there is one thing that I have to know. Please tell me how, at your age, you are always three paces ahead of me wherever we go?" I will never forget her answer. "I don't go in my own strength," she said. "I go in the strength of the Lord."

Bertha Smith continued to go in the strength of the Lord until she died at 101 years of age. This was a woman who had learned a secret! And as I continued to talk with her about this idea of going in God's strength over the years, she continued to point me to Paul's words in Philippians 4:13, which is the passage I want to focus on for the rest of this lesson.

Here is what the apostle Paul wrote: "I can do all things through Christ who strengthens me." Now, that is a short verse, but I believe it reveals two important points that you need to understand as you seek to develop and maintain a servant's heart within God's kingdom. The first of these is that you can absolutely have confidence in Christ and His strength. But the second is that you can only do so as long as you remain within the boundaries of this promise. We will dig more fully into these two ideas as we move through this lesson.

3. "Be strong in the Lord and in the power of His might" (Ephesians 6:10). What does it mean to be strong in the Lord? What does that look like in your life?

4. What are some areas where you are currently relying only on your own strength?

CONFIDENCE IN CHRIST'S STRENGTH

Paul actually makes a staggering statement in Philippians 4:13: "I can do all things through Christ who strengthens me." At first glance, it seems that Paul is declaring that he can do *anything*—that he can accomplish anything. This would be quite a boast.

However, when we look at this verse in the original Greek language, we see a different emphasis. Another way to translate Paul's words that line up more closely to the Greek would look something like this: "All things I am enabled to do through the strength of Christ." The key is the idea of being *enabled*. Paul is not claiming his ability to do all things in his own power. He understood he had no power in and of himself. Rather, the power came from Christ. The same is true for us as we seek to serve in God's kingdom. We will only be successful in our service to the extent that we serve as people enabled or empowered by God.

What I am saying is that there are limits to Paul's promise in this verse. It is not true that we can "do all things." It is only true that we can "do all things through Christ." Why is this? Primarily because God doesn't *want* us to do all things. We like to say, "God has a plan for my life," and that is quite true. His plan involves empowering us to accomplish the tasks He sets before us. However, there are many times we want to be rock-star Christians, and so we take on more than we can handle—and more than God *wants* us to handle. We then feel confused about why we are so worn out and weary. The reason is because we are claiming to trust God even as we are taking matters into our own hands and setting our own agenda.

This simply will not work. But here is the good news: when we stay within the boundaries of what Christ strengthens us to accomplish, we can accomplish an incredible amount for Him. We can have confidence that His strength will be more than enough to carry us through any obstacle that stands against His will. Just look at the apostle Paul if you need an example. Here is how he described his life to the Christians in Corinth:

> From the Jews five times I received forty stripes minus one. Three times I was beaten with rods; once I was stoned; three times I was shipwrecked; a night and a day I have been in the deep; in journeys often, in perils of waters, in perils of robbers, in perils of my own countrymen, in perils of the Gentiles, in perils in the city, in perils in the wilderness, in perils in the sea, in perils among false brethren; in weariness and toil, in

sleeplessness often, in hunger and thirst, in fastings often, in cold and nakedness (2 Corinthians 11:24–27).

Paul endured an incredible amount of trials and tribulations during his life of service to God. Not only did he endure them, but he also *thrived* in his ministry in spite of those obstacles and those struggles. He accomplished much for the kingdom of God because he relied completely on Christ's strength, and not his own.

Furthermore, Paul wrote his letter to the Philippians while he was in prison. Yet he could still write, "Not that I speak in regard to need, for I have learned in whatever state I am, to be content: I know how to be abased, and I know how to abound. Everywhere and in all things I have learned both to be full and to be hungry, both to abound and to suffer need. I can do all things through Christ who strengthens me" (Philippians 4:11–13).

Don't miss the importance of what Paul is saying here. Everything he wrote about strength, everything he wrote about content-ment, everything he wrote about God supplying his needs—it was all wrapped up in the truth that Jesus was the center of Paul's life. May the same be true of you and me.

5. Do you feel confident that God will empower you each day? Explain.

6. How would you assess your ability to stay within the guideline of only accomplishing what God leads you to accomplish?

_____

_____

_____

_____

_____

_____

_____

_____

_____

POSITION, PERSPECTIVE, AND PROMISES

One of the reasons Paul felt so confident in declaring, "I can do all things through Christ," is that he knew and understood his *position* in Christ. This position is the same one that all Christians enjoy, and yet many believers live their whole lives and never understand it. Many times they don't even hear about this position and are not aware of it.

What is our position in Christ? It is simply this: *we are weak and He is strong.* We do not have what it takes to do the work in front of us—and we never will. We are limited. We are fragile. We are ill-equipped. That's the bad news. But the good news is that God is strong. He is unlimited. He is all-powerful. And He is infinitely able to equip us with everything we need.

When you received Jesus as your Savior, the Bible says that Christ—through the Holy Spirit—came to indwell you. This means a person of the Trinity, a person of the Godhead, is now at home within your spirit. God Himself is living within you. For what reason? To empower you to do all that God requires and all that He desires. God indwells you so you can become everything He wants you to be and to do everything He wants you to do. He is not sitting on the outside but is on the inside. This is our position in Christ.

Not only did Paul understand his *position* in Christ, but he also had the right *perspective* of Christ. He understood the nature and character of Jesus. As he wrote to the Colossians, "[Jesus] is the image of the invisible God, the firstborn over all creation. For by Him all things were created that are in heaven and that are on earth, visible and invisible, whether thrones or dominions or principalities or powers. All things were created through Him and for Him. And He is before all things, and in Him all things consist" (Colossians 1:15–17).

Paul understood that Jesus is omnipotent (all-powerful), omniscient (all-knowing), omnipresent (present everywhere), and supreme not just over our little corner of the world, but also over the entire universe. Paul understood that Jesus' power and Jesus' resources are inexhaustible. Therefore, he knew that he could do "all things through Christ."

Finally, Paul had a firm understanding of God's promises. He knew, for example, that God promised to His people, "Those who wait on the Lord shall renew their strength; they shall mount up with wings like eagles, they shall run and not be weary, they shall walk and not faint" (Isaiah 40:31). Paul wanted others to understand the incredible nature of God's promises, which is why he prayed, "[May] the eyes of your understanding [be] enlightened; that you may know what is the hope of His calling, what are the riches of the glory of His inheritance in the saints, and what is the exceeding greatness of His power toward us who believe, according to the working of His mighty power" (Ephesians 1:18–19).

God is strengthening you and empowering you to overcome any and every situation you might face in service to Him. Now, this doesn't mean you will never get physically tired. It doesn't mean you will never feel momentarily worn out or frustrated or confused. But it does mean that you will never get tired of serving Jesus. When you rely on His strength and enabling power, you will be able to continue moving forward even when others drop out.

7. Do you have a firm understanding of your position in Christ? Does your life reflect that position?

....

....

....

....

....

....

8. Which of God's promises in His Word have been important to you recently? Why?

....

....

....

....

....

TAPPING IN

Let's end this lesson with the big question. I know it is one that has been on your mind for some time now: *How do I tap into this source of power so that I can get God's energy, His empowerment, moving in my life immediately?* Well, this is the same question that I had for Bertha Smith. I knew my position in Christ, and I understood God's promises from the Bible, but I still didn't know if I was experiencing His power the way I should.

So I asked her, "How do you tap into God's strength?" Her answer was so simple. She said, "Here's what I do. When I am serving the Lord in some area and I begin to feel weary or tired, I just pause and remind Him of what He promised me. I tell Him that I am—

at this moment—drawing from His resources exactly what I need. And then I draw it by faith."

Just two simple steps: remind God of His promises, and then draw His power through faith. I think we are all good at the first part. We all know how to remind God of what we think He is supposed to be doing in our lives. "God, You told me I would have everything I need." "You told me I would run and not grow faint." "You told me I would have access to Your Spirit and be connected to You like a branch is connected to a vine—so why am I still so worn out?" It is the second step where we need to improve. We need to draw God's power through faith. In other words, we need to draw God's power by *acting* in faith. By taking a step of faith.

You are going to get tired as you serve God and work in His kingdom. You may even feel worn out. But as Bertha Smith said, this is the moment when you need to remind God of His promises and draw His strength. However, you don't then wait until you feel strong and resume your service on God's behalf. That is not faith! Rather, you draw God's strength by *continuing to serve even when you are tired*, and in doing so you actively demonstrate your trust in God.

This is how you tap into His power: by acting in faith. This is how God worked in Abraham's life—through faith. This is how God worked in Joshua's life and David's life and Paul's life. Jesus Christ is the same yesterday, today, and forever, and He will work to empower your life when you step out in faith.

9. In what areas of life are you feeling weary or worn thin?

10. What will it look like for you to step out in faith and trust in the presence of God's power this coming week?

....

....

....

....

....

....

TODAY AND TOMORROW

Today: I don't have to serve God or accomplish His will through my own strength—in fact, I can't.

Tomorrow: I will step out in faith and trust that God's power will see me through whatever comes my way.

CLOSING PRAYER

Heavenly Father, we thank You for the wonderful example of the apostle Paul. We see from his life that there will be times when we will endure great trials and difficulties in our service to You. During such times, let us never seek to rely on our own strength, but draw us to You as the ultimate source of our power and comfort. Thank You for the promise that we do not have to grow weary, get worn down, and be discouraged and disillusioned, because we can rely on You as our fountain of life. We commit today to look to You as the source of all that we need, knowing that all we have to do is to believe You with a simple childlike faith.

Notes and Prayer Requests

. . . .

Use this space to write any key points, questions, or prayer requests from this week's study.

SERVING THROUGH SPIRITUAL GIFTS

IN THIS LESSON

Learning: What do Christians mean when they talk about spiritual gifts?

Growing: How can I serve God through my own spiritual gift?

As we've seen several times throughout this study, we are most effective in serving God when we rely on His strength rather than our own. Conversely, we are least effective in making a difference in our world and God's kingdom when our efforts are based on our abilities, our talents, our resources, and so on. In other words, developing a servant's heart is about developing a reliance on God and determining how to be equipped through His strength.

In this lesson, we will examine how one of the best ways for us to make sure our service is God-fueled is to serve through the lens of our spiritual gifts rather than through the resources and abilities of our flesh. Now, I know that "spiritual gifts" is a term that scares some people. But we should not be scared. In fact, we should be thrilled, because the spiritual gifts were always intended to be blessings in our lives. They were intended to help us actively serve and produce fruit as members of God's kingdom.

1. What is the first thing that comes to mind when you hear the phrase *spiritual gifts*?

....

....

....

....

....

....

2. How would you describe the idea of spiritual gifts to someone who had never heard of them?

....

....

....

....

....

....

ALL CHRISTIANS HAVE A SPIRITUAL GIFT

Before we go any further, it is important to debunk one particular myth that I have heard again and again as a pastor. What I am talking about is when believers in Christ say, "I don't have a spiritual gift." Yes, you do. All Christians have a spiritual gift.

Thankfully, you do not have to take my word on this fact. All you need to do is acknowledge the truth of God's Word: "As each one has received a gift, minister it to one another, as good stewards of the manifold grace of God" (1 Peter 4:10). Peter makes it clear in this verse that "each one has received a gift." This means that every person who has experienced the indwelling of the Holy Spirit—every person who has received salvation through faith in Jesus Christ—has also received a gift from that same Holy Spirit.

These gifts are not *talents*, such as the ability to dunk a basketball or to whiz through complicated math problems in your head. Talents are innate abilities and interests that can be developed from a young age. Nor are these gifts *ministries*, such as serving as an usher, helping on the welcoming team at the church, or providing childcare for toddlers on Wednesday night. Ministries are opportunities for service in the church based on the needs in the congregation.

Rather, *spiritual gifts* are internal drives or motivations that God has given you for use in building up His kingdom. This is why they are often referred to as "motivational gifts." Specifically, a spiritual gift is a special ability that God gives to believers in Christ to carry out the work that He has called them to do. Another way to say it is that a spiritual gift is a specific capacity for service given by God without regard to merit—meaning that spiritual gifts are not something we earn or achieve. They are *gifts*.

Thankfully, the apostle Paul provides a clear list of what those gifts are and how they can be applied within the church to great effect: "Having then gifts differing according to the grace that is given to us, let us use them: if prophecy, let us prophesy in proportion to our faith; or ministry, let us use it in our ministering; he who teaches, in teaching; he who exhorts, in exhortation; he who gives, with liberality; he who leads, with diligence; he who shows mercy, with cheerfulness" (Romans 12:6–8).

Notice there are seven spiritual or motivational gifts in this passage that Paul specifically calls out: prophecy, ministry (or service), teaching, exhorting (or encouraging), giving, leadership (or administration), and mercy. If you are a follower of Christ, then you *have* been given one of those gifts. You received it at the same moment you received the Holy Spirit inside you as Comforter and Advocate. Furthermore, you were given that gift for a reason—and you need to use it within God's kingdom. This is one of the ways you develop a servant's heart.

3. How confident do you feel when it comes to identifying your spiritual gifts?

4. What comes to mind as examples of models for specific gifts? For example, who is a model of teaching? Leadership? Mercy?

SERVE BY DISCOVERING YOUR SPIRITUAL GIFTS

There are three primary ways that you can serve God through your spiritual gifts. *The first is simply by discovering what are your spiritual gifts.* All Christians are called to serve God through the application of their spiritual gifts in the church and in the world—so it creates a problem when Christians don't know what their spiritual gifts might be. So, one of the biggest steps you can take toward developing a servant's heart is discovering your gifts—and doing so quickly.

The key to discovering your spiritual gift is to ask yourself this question: *"Why am I doing this?"* In other words, what is your motivation? You won't discover your spiritual gifts by asking, *"What should I do?"* or, *"What am I supposed to do?"* Nor will you discover them by continually stewing on the question, *"What are my gifts?"* Instead, you need to dig deeper and look at the motivations behind your actions and your feelings—to find the *why*.

For example, let's say you always feel wonderful when you have the opportunity to meet someone's need. When you encounter someone who has a debt, it feels amazing to pay it off, whether the person knows you did it or not. When you have an opportunity to clean house each spring, you don't really enjoy the cleaning and the organizing, but you do feel excited about bagging up the extra clothes and toys and taking them to a donation center. In this case, you are a prime candidate for the gift of *giving*, because you are driven by the desire to give.

Or maybe you consistently feel motivated by the desire to teach. When you spend time with your children, you look for opportunities to teach them something new. Or in your job, you like it when new employees come along and ask questions—it gives you the chance to answer them. In that case, you likely have the gift of *teaching*.

There are all kinds of assessments and evaluations out there that are designed to help Christians identify their spiritual gifts. These certainly have value, but really discovering your spiritual gifts doesn't have to be difficult. If you prayerfully take a look at your inner motivations—at what drives you day in and day out—you will soon have a firm idea about the spiritual gifts that you have received from God.

5. How would you describe the core motivations or drives within your heart?

....

....

....

....

....

....

....

....

6. What would you identify as your spiritual gifts? Why?

....

....

....

....

....

....

....

....

SERVE BY DEVELOPING
YOUR SPIRITUAL GIFTS

Once you have discovered your spiritual gifts, the next step is to help those gifts to grow and strengthen within you. People are often surprised when I say this, because they believe that gifts are static—that they don't change. They say, "Someone with the gift of mercy looks for opportunities to be merciful and show kindness to others. It's just part of who they are."

This is true in a sense. But it is also true that someone who has a natural talent for athletics can play sports and even excel in specific sporting events without expending much effort. However, that same person can also *develop* that talent. They can work hard on the practice field or on the court. They can strengthen their muscles in the gym and increase their flexibility. They can study film and drill themselves in movements over and over again to build muscle memory. Why would they do this? To develop their athletic talent and make it stronger.

In the same way, you also develop your spiritual gifts. You can make them stronger. In fact, you *should* make them stronger, for doing so will increase their potency and their effectiveness within the church. Be aware, however, that you cannot develop spiritual gifts in a natural way. By this, I mean that you cannot develop your spiritual gifts in the same way athletes develop their physical talent— through exercise, and repetition, and so on.

Instead, spiritual gifts need to be developed and grown in a spiritual way. You will only develop your spiritual gifts to the degree that you learn how to walk in the Holy Spirit. Always remember that your spiritual gifts were given by the Holy Spirit inside you. Your gifts are fueled and empowered by the Holy Spirit. Therefore, you must rely on the Holy Spirit to grow and develop those gifts.

First and foremost, this means examining your life, repenting of anything that should not be there—any form of sin or the consequences of sin—and then making an intentional choice to submit to God. You can start by praying, "Lord, I give You permission to do anything You choose in my life and through my life. I am a follower of Jesus and I know my own helplessness; therefore, I choose to rely on the Holy Spirit to empower me. I give You permission to use me and guide me as You see fit."

Why is this necessary? Because if you are not walking in the Spirit, you are walking in the flesh. You are attempting to use your gifts and serve God out of your human strength and your own limited resources—which is bound to fail. You can only develop your spiritual gifts through submission to God and His Holy Spirit.

Once you are walking in the power of the Holy Spirit, *then* you can seek to develop your gifts by more traditional means. You can learn the characteristics of your gifts—perhaps by reading articles or books that help you to better understand them. And you can find situations and opportunities that will help you practice those gifts. But again, those methods will only benefit you when you approach them through the power of the Holy Spirit.

7. What is a talent or ability you have worked to develop?

8. What are some first steps you can take to "walk in the power of the Spirit" rather than your own strength?

SERVE BY EXERCISING YOUR GIFTS

A final way to serve God through your spiritual gifts is by exercising those gifts. Two statistics often presented about Christians that make me feel sad is that (1) twenty percent of believers in the church give about eighty percent of the money within the church, and (2) twenty percent of Christians in the church do about eighty percent of the work to keep things running.

This means that on any given Sunday at a typical church, about eighty percent of the people there are *spectators*. They are not participating in any meaningful way but are simply along for the ride. However, when you look at the Scriptures—especially the passages that deal with spiritual gifts—it is clear that there is no provision for spectators in God's kingdom. Instead, *all* are called to be active in working to advance that kingdom within the world.

As the apostle Paul wrote, "Having then gifts differing according to the grace that is given to us, let us use them" (Romans 12:6). Peter also wrote to the early church, "As each one has received a gift, minister it to one another, as good stewards of the manifold grace of God" (1 Peter 4:10). All Christians need to ask themselves from time to time and season to season, *"Am I a spectator? Am I sitting up in the stands while people work to advance God's kingdom—and maybe even criticizing them? Or I am in the game, making things happen?*

Remember, if you are a believer in Christ, the Bible says you *have* been given a special gift from God. If you want to serve God in any meaningful way, you need to discover that gift. Not only that, but you need to develop that gift—to grow in it. And then, most importantly, you need to exercise that gift. You need to give yourself away to others through that gift so you can become a good steward "of the manifold grace of God." Otherwise, you are outside of God's will as a Christian. You are living in the flesh, living in carnality, and disobeying God.

But if you have discovered the joy of serving Christ through your spiritual gifts—of exercising those gifts for Him and others—then you don't have to worry about being a spectator. Because it is joy indeed. And you will want more. So never forget that within you is a dynamic, supernatural, incredible gift that was given by God Himself. When you choose to actively use that gift in service to God, you will release that amazing potential and see the wonderful fruit of blessings passed on to people by the hundreds and even thousands.

Maybe you think, *"I could never impact thousands."* Never put limitations on what God can do. You won't have the power to impact that many people for good, but that is exactly the point—God has that power. And He has planted that power inside you in the form of a spiritual gift. Therefore, when you obediently exercise that gift to honor Him, there are no limits to what can be accomplished. There are no limits to your impact on this world and the next.

9. Where do you see an opportunity to exercise your spiritual gift in the coming weeks?

10. Where do you see opportunities to help others identify, develop, and use their spiritual gifts within your church and community?

TODAY AND TOMORROW

Today: I am commanded to discover, develop, and exercise
my spiritual gift as an act of obedience to God.

Tomorrow: When I use my spiritual gift to serve
God and others, there is no limit to what can
be accomplished for God's kingdom.

CLOSING PRAYER

Father, in the name of Jesus we pray that the Holy Spirit will embed these principles into our hearts and minds. Grant us the wisdom to recognize that You have given each and every one of us a gift that You desire us to express to further the gospel. Help us to serve You today by first discovering those unique gifts. Enable us to continue to serve You by actively developing those gifts as You lead and direct. Finally, help us to heed Your call to action and exercise those gifts. Give us the courage to step up and become involved in the lives of others.

Notes and
Prayer Requests

Use this space to write any key points, questions, or prayer requests from this week's study.

THE REWARDS OF SERVICE

IN THIS LESSON

Learning: What reward can I expect from God?

Growing: How can I become worthy of reward?

God rewards service. Nothing that you will ever do in the name of Jesus for another person will go unrewarded by God. Of course, as we stated at the start of this study, we must be careful not to count our *salvation* as one of God's rewards for service. Salvation of one's soul is *not* a reward for our good deeds or our service. Rather, salvation is a free gift from God, motivated solely by His love for us. It is a "grace gift" that we cannot earn and that is never linked to our personal merit (see Ephesians 2:8–9).

What *is* linked to our service is the rewards that the Lord has for us—both in this life and in eternity. As the author of Hebrews states, "For God is not unjust to forget your work and labor of love which you have shown toward His name, in that you have ministered to the saints, and do minister" (Hebrews 6:10). We should never be motivated in our service by the potential for a reward—our motivation should be thanksgiving and love for God and obedience to His command to love our fellow man. But as we serve, we can be assured that God always takes note of our service and that He will reward it.

1. "Not by works of righteousness which we have done, but according to His mercy He saved us, through the washing of regeneration and renewing of the Holy Spirit" (Titus 3:5). Why should you not consider salvation a reward for living a godly life?

2. "For the Son of Man will come in the glory of His Father with His angels, and then He will reward each according to his works" (Matthew 16:27). What comes to mind when you consider being *rewarded* by God? What hope do you find in this promise?

OUR REWARD IS FROM GOD

When we serve others, we are serving the Lord. No matter whom we serve, God says that He is the beneficiary. As Paul states, we are "bondservants of Christ, doing the will of God from the heart, with goodwill doing service, as to the Lord, and not to men, knowing that whatever good anyone does, he will receive the same from the Lord, whether he is a slave or free" (Ephesians 6:6–8). It is Christ that we serve, and it is from Christ that we can expect our reward.

I learned this lesson early in my life as a young teenager delivering newspapers. Few of the people to whom I delivered newspapers saw me. They simply counted on their newspapers being there when they awoke. It wasn't easy to get up early and do that job—I don't know a teenage boy who wouldn't rather sleep than bundle newspapers and do a paper route. I did my job as unto the Lord, as if I were delivering *His* newspaper each morning.

It was while I was selling newspapers on a street corner that I met a man who was instrumental in my going to college to become a pastor. Was that an accident? I don't believe it was. I believe that God was rewarding those many hours of faithful service. That man was God's *instrument*, but it was from God that I received my reward.

It is to our advantage that our rewards come from God for two main reasons. *First, God alone knows precisely what we need and when we need it.* The Lord sees and anticipates our needs long in advance of our feeling or recognizing a need in our own lives, and He provides what is best for us. *Second, God alone can give rewards that are eternal.* Material rewards rust, rot, and wither. Recognition and applause are fleeting. God, in contrast, gives us a deep and abiding fulfillment on this earth, as well as rewards that extend into eternity.

3. "He who is faithful in what is least is faithful also in much; and he who is unjust in what is least is unjust also in much" (Luke 16:10). Why is it important to serve God with both the tasks that seem insignificant and also the ones that appear to hold great purpose?

....

....

....

....

....

....

....

....

4. Who is someone who has proven faithful in the little things in life? How have you seen God reward that person's efforts?

....

....

....

....

....

....

....

....

REWARDS COME IN DEGREES

God rewards all service, but He does not give out equal rewards for all service. A job may seem great or small from our perspective, but it is the *act* of service that God sees and rewards. Service is service . . . and God does not give differing rewards because one type of service is of greater or lesser importance than another. Rather, He gives differing rewards on the basis of *our heart motivation and our faithfulness in performing the act of service.*

Jesus once told His disciples a parable about servants who had received different amounts of money (or *talents*). The Lord will say to the servants who used their talents to the fullest, "Well done, good and faithful servant; you were faithful over a few things, I will make you ruler over many things. Enter into the joy of your lord" (Matthew 25:21, 23). The servants were not rewarded on the basis of the *amount* of money they were given, or *how* they invested their talents, but because they were "good and faithful servants." They performed their service as well as they knew how, and they were faithful and persevering.

Jesus also distinguished between rewards and *great* rewards, saying those who persevere in their service for the Lord in spite of persecution will receive a *great* reward (see Matthew 5:11–12) When Peter asked what reward he and the other disciples might expect from their faithfulness, Jesus replied, "Everyone who has left houses or brothers or sisters or father or mother or wife or children or lands, for My name's sake, shall receive a hundredfold, and inherit eternal life" (Matthew 19:29). Mark adds that Jesus said the faithful will receive "a hundredfold . . . with persecutions" (Mark 10:29–30).

Of course, the more God rewards you, the more Satan will be upset about your rewards. The enemy of your soul has no interest in seeing you blessed by God, so he will persecute you all the more as you receive greater and greater rewards from the Lord. However, the good news is that the more you are persecuted for your witness about Jesus Christ, the more your reward grows! The enemy's persecutions can never outdistance or overwhelm God's rewards on your life. You can be assured that the reward will always be greater than what you give. God multiplies your giving, no matter what form it takes.

When you give service to others, you are a sower of God's love and of the gospel of Jesus Christ (see Mark 4:3–8). So be encouraged in your service. At times you may see little or no progress in the lives of those you serve. You may feel as if all the good you are doing evaporates into thin air or is negated. But God says that at least *some* of your effort will succeed mightily. God is the One who grows your harvest. Keep on sowing!

5. "Blessed are you when they revile and persecute you, and say all kinds of evil against you falsely for My sake. Rejoice and be exceedingly glad, for great is your reward in heaven, for so they persecuted the prophets who were before you" (Matthew 5:11–12). Notice that Jesus adds the word *falsely* in this verse. Why is that distinction important?

....

....

....

....

....

....

....

6. In practical terms, how can you rejoice when you are suffering persecution?

....

....

....

....

....

....

....

....

DIFFERENT TYPES OF REWARDS

The Bible reveals there are different types of rewards for our service. *The first is tangible rewards.* Jesus said, "Give, and it will be given to you: good measure, pressed down, shaken together, and running over will be put into your bosom. For with the same measure that you use, it will be measured back to you" (Luke 6:38). God gives tangible rewards during this life.

Many of the gifts that God desires to give you will come through other people. You are responsible in such instances to give an accounting of your stewardship—how you use what you have been given. As Paul wrote, "Each of us shall give account of himself to God. Therefore let us not judge one another anymore, but rather resolve this, not to put a stumbling block or a cause to fall in our brother's way" (Romans 14:12–13). A person who gives you a reward is an agent of God's blessing—the Lord's *ways and means* of providing for you. Thank the person, but above all, thank God for the good reward that He has given to you.

Second, there are intangible rewards. The people in your world can also be agents of intangible rewards: praise, admiration, recognition, acknowledgment, and appreciation. It is not wrong to receive a sincere thank you from other people. What is wrong before God is when you serve Him and others out of a desire to receive accolades from others. Jesus was clear on this point, chiding the Pharisees for making a public display of their fasting, praying, and giving so they might appear to be righteous before men. Jesus said of them, "They have their reward" (Matthew 6:2). The Pharisees received the praise of others, but that was *all* they would receive. God was not in that reward.

Third, there are eternal rewards. Still other rewards that you receive from God will be eternal and will not be given until after you are in heaven. Jesus mentioned this type of reward when He said, "When you give a dinner or a supper, do not ask your friends, your brothers, your relatives, nor rich neighbors, lest they also invite you back, and you be repaid. But when you give a feast, invite the poor, the maimed, the lame, the blind. And you will be blessed, because they cannot repay you; for you shall be repaid at the resurrection of the just" (Luke 14:12–14). Furthermore, some rewards will not be given to us until we are resurrected. The Bible refers to at least four types of crowns that will be given to us for our service:

Crown	Those who will receive it
Imperishable crown	Those whose hearts' desires have been rooted in obedience (see 1 Corinthians 9:25)
Crown of life	Those who endure temptations, troubles, trials, and heartaches for Christ's sake (see James 1:12)
Crown of righteousness	Those who pour out their lives in service of the gospel (see 2 Timothy 4:8)
Crown of glory that does not fade away	Those who "feed the flock" (see 1 Peter 5:4)

None of us can truly grasp the glories of heaven. Nor can we begin to imagine or understand all of the blessings that God may have for us in eternity. The rewards the Lord has for us are immeasurable. None of us can possibly know all of the people that our lives have touched. Service to others has a ripple effect that goes beyond our ability to comprehend it. Each time I pick up an inspirational book, I am aware the author has blessed my life and served me. God will judge and reward each of us for the acts service that we have given.

Fourth, there are conditional rewards. Some of the rewards that you will receive from God are conditional and directly related to your obedience. Many of God's commandments are directly related to how you are to serve others. In the Old Testament, these commandments often related to widows, orphans, and strangers. Other commandments are related to how you serve God through your giving, sacrifices, and things you do for your fellow believers.

7. "I will . . . open for you the windows of heaven and pour out for you such blessing that there will not be room enough to receive it" (Malachi 3:10). What is implied by the imagery used in this verse, such as "open the windows of heaven" and "pour out"?

....

....

....

....

....

....

8. "Do not lay up for yourselves treasures on earth . . . but lay up for yourselves treasures in heaven, where neither moth nor rust destroys and where thieves do not break in and steal" (Matthew 6:19–20). What are the "treasures in heaven" that the Lord promises us? How do we "lay up" those treasures?

....

....

....

....

....

ALL IN GOD'S PERFECT TIMING

God chooses the reward that you will receive, and He also chooses *when* you will receive it. As just discussed, some rewards are immediate, some are in the future, and still others are granted in eternity. God has just the right time for every reward so that it has maximum effectiveness and benefit in a person's life and in the life of the larger body of Christ.

145

Any farmer will tell you that crops have different growing seasons. A fruit tree sapling may not produce a full harvest for several years. Garden vegetables, by comparison, produce a harvest in a matter of weeks. Trees that are farmed for lumber may take decades to harvest. Your role is not to *force* a reward or to insist that God give you a reward out of season.

In the parable of the Prodigal Son, the younger son in the story demanded his inheritance out of season and ended up squandering it all (see Luke 15:11–24). You are to trust God with patience (see Psalm 37). A harvest *will* come, but it will be in God's perfect timing. So this week, ask the Lord to help you trust Him for your rewards and wait on His timing. Learning to trust patiently is a great reward in its own right.

9. "Let us not grow weary while doing good, for in due season we shall reap if we do not lose heart. Therefore, as we have opportunity, let us do good to all, especially to those who are of the household of faith" (Galatians 6:9-10). What conditions must we meet if we are to "reap" a good harvest?

10. What does it mean to "lose heart" in our service? How can we guard against it?

TODAY AND TOMORROW

Today: Jesus assures me that I can trust God to reward my service—both now and later.

Tomorrow: This week, I will ask the Lord to help me trust Him in all things, including my future reward.

CLOSING PRAYER

Heavenly Father, we thank You for loving us. You have given us such clear instructions on what You expect from us. You have given us such comforting and reassuring declarations of the truth of Your acceptance of us and the rewards that You have prepared for us. We do not want to miss out on any of the blessings that You have prepared for us in this life and the next! Help us to be faithful and committed stewards of Your gifts. Help us to serve others as if we were doing it unto You, not looking for any affirmation here on earth, but only looking to You as our Source.

NOTES AND
PRAYER REQUESTS

Use this space to write any key points, questions, or prayer requests from this week's study.

LEADER'S GUIDE

Thank you for choosing to lead your group through this Bible study from Dr. Charles F. Stanley on *Developing a Servant's Heart*. The rewards of being a leader are different from those of participating, and it is our prayer that your own walk with Jesus will be deepened by this experience. During the twelve lessons in this study, you will be helping your group members explore key themes about how to effectively serve others and review questions that will encourage group discussion. There are multiple components in this section that can help you structure your lessons and discussion time, so please be sure to read and consider each one.

BEFORE YOU BEGIN

Before your first meeting, make sure your group members each have a copy of *Developing a Servant's Heart* so they can follow along in the study guide and have their answers written out ahead of time. Alternately, you can hand out the study guides at your first meeting and give the group members some time to look over the material and ask any preliminary questions. During your first meeting, be sure to send a sheet around the room and have the members write down their name, phone number, and email address so you can keep in touch with them during the week.

To ensure everyone has a chance to participate in the discussion, the ideal size for a group is around eight to ten people. If there are more than ten people, break up the bigger group into smaller subgroups. Make sure the members are committed to participating each week, as this will help create stability and help you better prepare the structure of the meeting.

At the beginning of each meeting, you may wish to start the group time by asking the group members to provide their initial reactions to the material they have read during the week. The goal is to just get the group members' preliminary thoughts—so encourage them at this point to keep their answers brief. Ideally, you want everyone in the group to get a chance to share some of their thoughts, so try to keep the responses to a minute or less.

Give the group members a chance to answer, but tell them to feel free to pass if they wish. With the rest of the study, it's generally not a good idea to have everyone answer every question—a free-flowing discussion is more desirable. But with the opening icebreaker questions, you can go around the circle. Encourage shy people to share, but don't force them. Also, try to keep any one person from dominating the discussion so everyone will have the opportunity to participate.

WEEKLY PREPARATION

As the group leader, there are a few things you can do to prepare for each meeting:

- *Be thoroughly familiar with the material in the lesson.* Make sure you understand the content of each lesson so you know how to structure the group time and are prepared to lead the group discussion.

- *Decide, ahead of time, which questions you want to discuss.* Depending on how much time you have each week, you may not be able to reflect on every question. Select specific questions that you feel will evoke the best discussion.

- *Take prayer requests.* At the end of your discussion, take prayer requests from your group members and then pray for one another.

- *Pray for your group.* Pray for your group members throughout the week and ask God to lead them as they study His Word.

- *Bring extra supplies to your meeting.* The members should bring their own pens for writing notes, but it's a good idea to have extras available for those who forget. You may also want to bring paper and additional Bibles.

STRUCTURING THE GROUP DISCUSSION TIME

You will need to determine with your group how long you want to meet each week so you can plan your time accordingly. Generally, most groups like to meet for either sixty minutes or ninety minutes, so you could use one of the following schedules:

SECTION	60 Minutes	90 Minutes
WELCOME (group members arrive and get settled)	5 minutes	10 minutes
ICEBREAKER (group members share their initial thoughts regarding the content in the lesson)	10 minutes	15 minutes
DISCUSSION (discuss the Bible study questions you selected ahead of time)	35 minutes	50 minutes
PRAYER/CLOSING (pray together as a group and dismiss)	10 minutes	15 minutes

As the group leader, it is up to you to keep track of the time and keep things moving according to your schedule. If your group is having a good discussion, don't feel the need to stop and move on to the next question. Remember, the purpose is to pull together ideas and share unique insights on the lesson. Encourage everyone to participate, but don't be concerned if certain group members are more quiet. They may just be internally reflecting on the questions and need time to process their ideas before they can share them.

GROUP DYNAMICS

Leading a group study can be a rewarding experience for you and your group members—but that doesn't mean there won't be challenges. Certain members may feel uncomfortable in discussing topics that they consider very personal and might be afraid of being called on. Some members might have disagreements on specific issues. To help prevent these scenarios, consider establishing the following ground rules:

- If someone has a question that may seem off topic, suggest that it is discussed at another time, or ask the group if they are okay with addressing that topic.

- If someone asks a question to which you do not know the answer, confess that you don't know and move on. If you feel comfortable, you can invite the other group members to give their opinions or share their comments based on personal experience.

- If you feel like a couple of people are talking much more than others, direct questions to people who may not have shared yet. You could even ask the more dominating members to help draw out the quiet ones.

- When there is a disagreement, encourage the members to process the matter in love. Invite members from opposing sides to evaluate their opinions and consider the ideas of the other members. Lead the group through Scripture that addresses the topic, and look for common ground.

When issues arise, encourage your group to follow these words from Scripture: "Love one another" (John 13:34), "If it is possible, as much as it depends on you, live peaceably with all men" (Romans 12:18), "Whatever things are true...noble...pure...lovely...if there is any virtue and if there is anything praiseworthy—meditate on these things" (Philippians 4:8), and "Be swift to hear, slow to speak, slow to wrath" (James 1:19). This will make your group time more rewarding and beneficial for everyone who attends.

Thank you again for your willingness to lead your group. May God reward your efforts and dedication, equip you to guide your group in the weeks ahead, and make your time together in *Developing a Servant's Heart* fruitful for His kingdom.

Also Available in the
Charles F. Stanley Bible Study Series

The Charles F. Stanley Bible Study Series is a unique approach to Bible study, incorporating biblical truth, personal insights, emotional responses, and a call to action. Each study draws on Dr. Stanley's many years of teaching the guiding principles found in God's Word, showing how we can apply them in practical ways to every situation we face. This edition of the series has been completely revised and updated, and includes two brand-new lessons from Dr. Stanley.

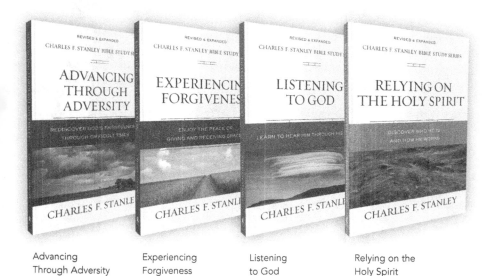

Advancing Through Adversity	Experiencing Forgiveness	Listening to God	Relying on the Holy Spirit
9780310106555	9780310106579	9780310106593	9780310106616

Available now at your favorite bookstore.
More volumes coming soon.

THOMAS NELSON
Since 1798